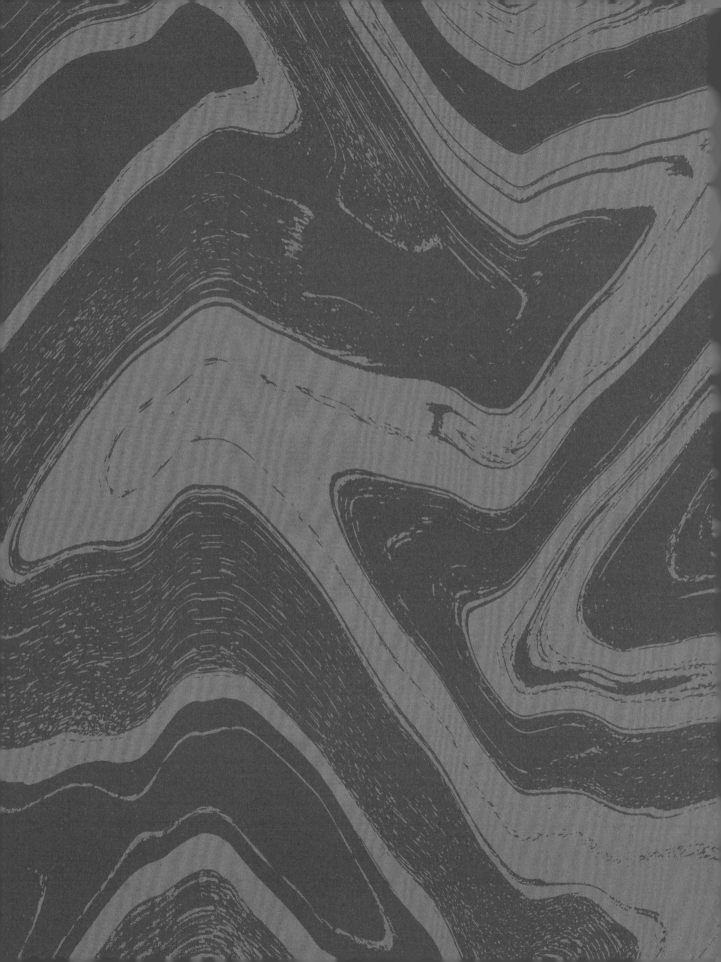

THE CHOI
OF COOKING

THE choi OF COOKING

Flavor-Packed, Rule-Breaking Recipes for a Delicious Life

Roy Choi

with Tien Nguyen & Natasha Phan

PHOTOGRAPHS BY BOBBY FISHER
ILLUSTRATIONS BY ADELA QERSAQI

 CLARKSON POTTER/
PUBLISHERS
NEW YORK

CLARKSON POTTER/PUBLISHERS
An imprint of the Crown Publishing Group
A division of Penguin Random House LLC
clarksonpotter.com

Library of Congress Cataloging-in-Publication Data is available upon request.

ISBN 978-0-593-57925-1
Ebook ISBN 978-0-593-57926-8

Printed in China

Editor: Jennifer Sit | Editorial assistant: Elaine Hennig
Designer: Laura Palese | Art director: Ian Dingman | Illustrator: Adela Qersaqi
Production editor: Serena Wang
Production manager: Phil Leung
Prepress color manager: Neil Spitkovsky
Compositor: Hannah Hunt
Food stylist: Caroline Hwang | Food stylist assistants: Jesse Ramirez and Sunny Cho
Prop stylist: Nidia Cueva | Prop stylist assistant: Eddie Barrera
Photo assistant: Dennis Lin | Digital tech: Alex Woods
Recipe developers: Kumi Megumi, Sunny Cho, and Todd Chang
Copyeditor: Kate Slate | Proofreaders: Rita Madrigal, Lisa Brousseau | Indexer: Jay Kreider
Publicist: Jina Stanfill and Kristin Casemore | Marketer: Chloe Aryeh

Graphics by True Grit Texture Supply copyright © 4, 6, 14, 20, 38, 42, 44, 46, 48, 50, 56, 58, 70, 88, 100, 102, 104, 106, 112, 128, 132, 150, 178, 200, 213, 224, 228, 242, 252, 254, 256

Illustrations on pages 1, 16, 33, 35, and 137 by Adela Qersaqi

10 9 8 7 6 5 4 3 2 1

First Edition

CONTENTS

Welcome to

THE CHOI OF COOKING

What you have in your hands

is a book of recipes. An awesome book of recipes, trust. But we're not stopping there. Because it's not just an awesome book of recipes the same way the *Tao of Jeet Kune Do* wasn't just a book about martial arts: Bruce Lee's manual was a book about life, about how to approach yourself and others around you. This book is my *Tao of Jeet Kune Do:* a book of life, a recipe to keep living and be alive. It will fill your life with flavors so vibrant, so good, it will possess you. It'll teach you how to make things that are good for you and good to you. It'll make you kiss yourself as your food kisses others—seriously it'll be that good.

I mean, that's the goal.

I've been cooking for you all for a while now, but it took me this long to write this book because it took me this long to live long enough to know I had something to give you. And that's what you have in your hands: my heart and my soul.

Off the top, this is a collection of fun dishes

with some thoughts about cooking and living along the way. Some are my takes on classics, others are created from a lifetime of cooking mash-ups. If all you want to do is make some fucking delicious food, I got you. It's all here. You can just skip all this ramble and preamble and dive right in. A Thai-inspired chowder? Page 138. Layers and layers of greens hugging slivers of pork belly? Page 218. Fish tacos? Check page 186.

But if you're still listening, let me tell you this story about how I got here.

I spent a long time wrestling with my food demons. Growing up and into my young adult days, I was on a whole other level of champion eating: bundles of Red Vines, gallon-sized milkshakes, whole pizzas, cans of SpaghettiOs, a dozen flour tortillas like they were potato chips, eight portions of soba noodles at a time. The whole tray of Stouffer's lasagna. I could pound four of those personal Pizza Hut pan pizzas at a time. Who actually eats the whole bread bowl in a clam chowder bread bowl? Me, that's who. And there is this thing in Korean called *ggokbaeggi*, which means "extra-large." Yup. Ggokbaeggi for your boy. All. The. Time. From pho to jjajangmyun.

Really, though, I was eating my feelings. An evil voice would taunt me when I looked at myself in the mirror, sending me straight to the pint of Häagen-Dazs. On some afternoons when I was so depressed I could barely get off the couch, I almost couldn't manage getting into the kitchen to microwave a pizza. Then, when I felt like I was getting too heavy, I just . . . didn't eat. Instead of eating, I went on benders. Other addictions replaced the food. Sometimes it was drugs; other times, the casinos. I seesawed; sometimes I relapsed and fell into an abyss and had to start all over again. But for the most part, I controlled my weight and eating by ricocheting between the extreme for many years. Because at the time, I thought that's what it meant to control your weight, to diet.

THIS BOO

K OF LIFE

After I moved away from the drugs and the gambling and started cooking professionally and coming up in kitchens, I was constantly on the move. My meals became bits of vegetables and spoonfuls of sauces here and there. I still had my demons, though—they never completely go away—and sometimes they'd get the better of me and I'd spit fire, cook angry, smoke fuming out of my ears, eyes locked in, slamming pan after pan on the sauté station, bam bam bam, then eating angry to feed an animalistic craving that roared from somewhere deep.

Being in restaurant kitchens is a lot like being at the casino: It can sometimes be like a time warp. You miss chunks of life while you're in that chamber. I missed all sorts of pop culture diets—cleansing, juicing, paleo, Atkins—but it's possible I might have been too stubborn to learn them anyway. I thought my way of eating on the go, eating whatever I thought my body was telling me to eat, then not eating when it got too much, was the way. I didn't understand that so much of what I was eating was just empty of any nutritional value and making me feel worse. At some point a few years ago, I was tipping the scales at 200-plus pounds, feeling unhealthy, hiding in my junk food abyss, falling into old habits, but trying to hold it all together with a broken smile in public.

I'm stubborn, but even then I knew my way wasn't working. Something had to give.

I made up my mind and looked to change up how I cook. I let my chef's intuition guide me to make stuff I crave and would eat any other day, but intentionally pulled back the meat and upped the vegetables and discovered ways to pull in rainbows of flavor. Big fucking salads with a simple Dijon mustard vinaigrette. Grilled fish with a ginger ponzu sauce. Tofu seared and outfitted with soy, scallions, and buttery kimchi. A noodle salad filled with veggies and draped in a gochujang sauce.

And the thing is, once I started cooking and eating like this, it stuck. When I cook and eat now, I'm usually thinking vegetables first. More herbs, more aromatics, less meat, less sugar. All almost without even thinking about it.

The recipes in this book are the result of that journey. It reflects the cooking I do now: vegetable-forward with pit stops of comfort along the way. Those pit stops of comfort are key: I still have my cravings. I know the pull of that burger, of a bomb Philly cheesesteak, of a Taiwanese-style pork chop lightly fried and

RATHER THAN PRETENDING LIKE OUR CRAVINGS DON'T EXIST, I'M GOING TO JUST ASK THAT YOU TREAT THEM RIGHT.

served over white rice. My philosophy isn't about denial. It's about balance. It's about being kind to yourself. And being kind means hugging the foods that hug us back.

So rather than pretending like our cravings don't exist, I'm going to just ask that you treat them right. When the demons come around to visit me, for example, and I need my greasy fix, then I've made a deal with myself: I'll eat a burger, but it's a burger that *I* make so I control every part of it. I'll treat it like it's my first and only burger, so I gotta make it a perfect bite because it'll be my only bite. This means getting the best ingredients I can to really maximize the flavor—and that means just a little bit will go a long way. So, whatever craving you have, put in the care and time to cook it up yourself. I'll show you how, and I promise it'll be more rewarding and better for you than hitting the drive-thru.

That's why even though this is a book about eating and treating yourself better, it isn't your typical "healthy" cookbook in that chicken nuggets probably don't line up with how our culture defines healthy. But fuck that. Healthy means different things depending on who you are. And I'm here to support you wherever you are in your journey.

Whatever we make together, it'll be full of flavor layered in each bite, flavors that come from all over. I'm a kid who grew up with one foot in one culture and the other foot in another yet who had to walk a blurred one-way path, intertwined like a trail in a fairytale forest. And I'm not the only one. I see all of you out there—immigrants, Americans, everyone—who were doing and *are* doing the same right now. So, as we work through these tacos and salads and soups, you'll see that a lot of dishes in this book are rooted in multiple places, and they're going to reflect their multiple starting points to create a whole new point on the map.

I'll also hit other dishes I grew up with but tweaked in a way that I would have done if I'd known then what I know now. That can mean something as simple as knowing when to be patient and not rush the cooking process so flavors can fully develop, loading a dish with a new sauce, or adjusting the portion size to satisfy cravings without falling back into the abyss. These are dishes that I would have made if I was the one in charge of writing the food in my childhood script. It just took till now to figure out who I really was to even write the lines.

It's about the food, but it's also *not* about the food.

As you cook through the book, you'll see it's about the food, but it's also *not* about the food. My hope is that through this book, you will learn how to cook. Not to follow a recipe, though that is part of learning how to cook. But learning how to cook is more than following a recipe and making the dish look exactly like the photo. It's empowering yourself with the tools to take control of what and how you approach the food in your life.

Cooking is tasting and learning what flavors you like. It's trusting yourself, having patience. It's making time to cook things right and not looking for shortcuts. It's bringing who you are into the kitchen, and what you take with you when you leave. It's sweating the small stuff. It's learning the rules, then questioning the rules. It's flow, it's movement, it's jazz. It's rolling with mistakes as you go, it's knowing *how* to roll with the mistakes as you go.

I've learned all those things through making mistakes and fucking up and falling down and getting back up again. I've spent the last few decades learning the rules of cooking, and then breaking those rules and combining those broken pieces to make a whole new piece. It's like the Watts Towers, but instead of found objects, my piece is built on scraps of my life experiences and approach to cooking. And by passing what I've learned to you, I hope you can learn those lessons, too, without needing to take the long way around. So, embedded in the recipes and throughout these pages are bits of guidance that expand on my cooking style and philosophy. Sometimes it'll be real practical, like when to use a blender versus a food processor, when to mince instead of chop. Sometimes it'll be about working with a specific ingredient. And sometimes it'll be about battling yourself to find yourself. I hope those moments will show you how to not get lost in the weeds even when you're in the weeds. And all those moments, the lessons, strategies, and ideas you'll absorb as you cook, will build and accumulate. Soon enough, you'll be able to riff off my recipes and make your own meals. You'll be able to nourish yourself—and others, too.

I lived it so you can live it.

THE CHOI OF COOKING

I'm what the youngsters call an OG now.

I never thought I'd get here and never imagined what I'd feel if I ever did. But being here now, it's not as embarrassing as I thought it would be. Sure, I'm old, but with age comes wisdom and that wisdom comes from experience. I have found a path where my mind is clear, my body is strong, my heart radiates.

Remember what I said? *The Choi of Cooking* is a life book. My *Tao of Jeet Kune Do.*

After all these years, I learned that the best cooking comes from a place of love and kindness and generosity for yourself, the ingredients you cook, and those you feed. I know this is gonna change your life because the food in this book changed mine and all those who I feed every day. No cap.

And that's all because you trusted me, you trusted yourself. You applied technique, allowed yourself to make mistakes, embraced flavor, took your time, had a sense of humor about things, escaped the rat race, made peace with the demons, and made music for your soul through cooking.

So what do you say, are you ready for this?

**Let's go.
Roy**

GUIDING LIGHTS

There are no hard-and-fast rules to my cooking philosophy. Just a few guiding lights as you cook:

- Love for others and yourself
- Kindness in your heart
- Generosity of spirit and giving
- Flavor for days
- FUN FUN FUN
- Vibrancy and vibes
- Health is wealth
- Realness of intention
- Care of earth, technique, and detail
- Happiness is feeding

Find **YOUR O**

Whether you're new to cooking, you want to eat better than you do now, or you don't need anyone to convince you about the magic of vegetables, *The Choi of Cooking* is for you. And wherever you are, I'll meet you there with a few dishes to continue the journey.

Find yourself here:

If you're a couch potato

If your every day is filled with chips and Red Vines and extra-large everything and you want to take control of what you eat, you can do it. I know it, because I was there once, too. We're going to take one step at a time. Ease into a new direction with a smoothie or Agua Fresca (page 48). Throw together my Tuna Salad Niçoise Bibimbap (page 92). Roll up a Bean and Cheese Burrito (page 86). When the fast-food craving hits, make yourself a burger or some chicken nuggets (pages 239 and 208).

If you're a bit hesitant, with a toe in the water

If you want to take control of what you eat, but you're not yet super comfortable in the kitchen, start with a few simple and delicious recipes. Make one of the salsas (pages 250–251) or roast some carrots with garlic (page 74). Serve yourself some tofu with a soy-ginger sauce (page 114), then blend up my Magic Sauce (page 247) and spoon it over a bowl of cold noodles (page 152). Make a rice ball or a rice bowl (pages 168 and 164). Practice patience with my Korean Steamed Egg Soufflé (page 124) or Crispy Mashed Potatoes (page 82).

3 If you're on your way to eating better

If you already heart vegetables, a few ideas to add to your Tuesday night dinners: Grilled Romaine with Creamy Blue Cheese Dressing (page 94), Hot Chow Chow (page 72), Stir-Fried Pea Shoots (page 68), Roasted Cauliflower Steaks with Harissa and Garlic Herbed Butter (page 78).

4 If you were on your way to eating better, but you relapsed

If you were on the healthy path but went off road, a Green Juice (page 51), Oxtail Brisket Soup (page 146), Kimchi Tuna Melt Boats (page 182), Veggie on the Lo Mein Spaghetti (page 158), some crudités (page 56) or laab (page 96) will get you back on track.

5 If you're ready to play jazz like Coltrane

If you want to scale back the meat or carbs in your diet, riff on my recipes the same way a great jazz player swims between the notes after mastering the fundamentals. You can, for example, play around with the ratio of green beans to chicken in my stir-fry (page 202), swap out the meat for tofu in dishes like my Bomb Kha Chowder (page 138), or try beans instead of noodles in pasta dishes like my Shakshuka Baked Ziti (page 160).

6 If you're a namaste warrior

If your week is already a balanced mix of health and comfort, take this book and follow your eyes and stomach to mix and match: Have the Kimchi Steak Tacos (page 234) for lunch, say, and Crispy.Salmon. Lemon. (page 192) for dinner. A Big Fucking Salad (page 90) for lunch, Hawaiian-Style Garlic Shrimp (page 194) for dinner. You get the idea.

A NO
OON
RECI

TE THE PES

A few quick pointers about the recipes in this book

SERVING SIZES

Servings sizes in cookbooks and recipes are a trip, because everyone's idea of a serving size is wildly different. It's even different from meal to meal, day to day, whether you're feeling super hangry or whether you're feeling super low. So, take the serving sizes in this book as guidelines and combine them with your own experiences and inner voice to tell you if you'll need more to feed you and your crew or family.

SLICING & DICING & CHOPPING & MINCING

Depending on the dish, some ingredients will need to be chopped, others will need to be much more finely cut into a mince. These differences in how big or small you cut the ingredient might seem like a small thing, but there is intention there. How you prepare a clove of garlic or a bunch of cilantro, for example, makes a big difference in the flavor in the final dish. If we're going to blend everything to make a salsa (pages 250–251), say, I'll suggest that you chop it up in big pieces and let the blender do the work for you so you can focus your time, attention, and energy on stuff that needs your time, attention, and energy. On the other hand, if infusing an oil with garlic, like for my clam pasta (page 154), you need to cut the garlic into thin slivers. Go any smaller like a mince and the garlic won't hold up in the time and heat that it takes for all its flavors to fully extract, and you'll end up with a muddy, cloudy, sometimes even bitter flavor profile.

On the *other* other hand, where I'm looking for a quick, concentrated release of flavor to combine with other flavors, like in a stir-fry (page 202), or to meld the flavors into a broth, like in a chowder (page 138), I'm going to mince the garlic. It all just depends. And paying attention to these minuscule details can make the difference between a dish you just like and a dish you love.

EXTRA EXTRAS

At the end of a lot of the recipes, you'll find an extra tidbit or two about a few ways you can spin a recipe. These are labeled:

POWER UP

I share some favorite comfort foods in these pages, all of which satisfy when cravings grip you from somewhere deep. When you're ready, modify those recipes in ways that will make them even better for you. Those modifications are labeled Power Up.

GET IN WHERE YOU FIT IN

These are moments in this book where you can customize a dish with whatever you want to throw in, or where you can swap out what I use for something else that would suit you better. Get in where you fit in!

BONUS ROUNDS

There are a bunch of recipes in here, especially in the Souper Soups chapter, where you may end up with leftovers . . . which is exactly where you're supposed to end up, because that's just the way the dish is made. So, those recipes really aren't just for one dish; they're multiverses that hold countless possibilities. Ideas for how to transform those leftovers into something entirely new or to use them as a base for other dishes are labeled Bonus Rounds.

SWEATPANTS VERSION

There are a few recipes that take a little bit of extra time to put together, because sometimes you can't cheat code your way to getting it done sooner or with less prep. But, for recipes where there is a way to shorten the process so you can throw on your sweatpants, make a quick, low-effort meal, and chill out, I've highlighted the methods as Sweatpants Versions.

CHOICE WORDS

Every once in a while throughout the book, we'll sit down and take a breath and I'll tell you a story about a recipe, about cooking, about my zigzag journey. Those are Choice Words.

You Are Your Pantry, Your Pantry Is You

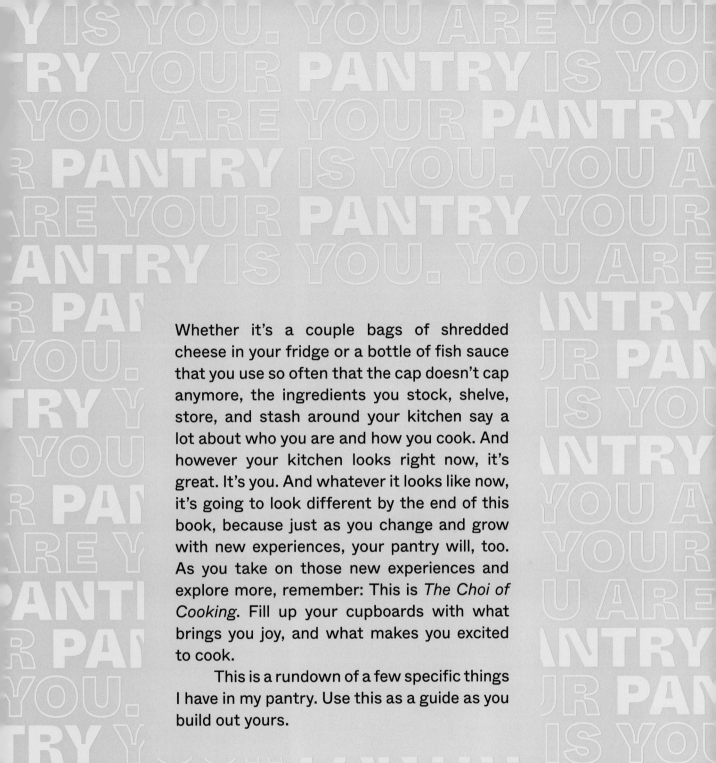

Whether it's a couple bags of shredded cheese in your fridge or a bottle of fish sauce that you use so often that the cap doesn't cap anymore, the ingredients you stock, shelve, store, and stash around your kitchen say a lot about who you are and how you cook. And however your kitchen looks right now, it's great. It's you. And whatever it looks like now, it's going to look different by the end of this book, because just as you change and grow with new experiences, your pantry will, too. As you take on those new experiences and explore more, remember: This is *The Choi of Cooking*. Fill up your cupboards with what brings you joy, and what makes you excited to cook.

This is a rundown of a few specific things I have in my pantry. Use this as a guide as you build out yours.

Aromatics

Anytime you start cooking and your tummy begins to grumble, or someone wanders into the kitchen because *it just smells so good*, it's probably because you added aromatics to the pan. Aromatics include ginger, garlic, scallions, lemongrass, onions, chile peppers, galangal, bay leaves, celery, carrots—basically, power ingredients that unleash the most amazing fragrances as they cook. They create the foundation of flavor for the dish. Once you can smell these aromatics, you know their flavors are flowing into the pan.

We use a ton of aromatics in this book, so I won't list them all here. But I do have a few notes on the ones I use the most:

GARLIC

I use garlic a lot. *A lot.* Other than pulsing peeled cloves a few times in a food processor to mince them, there really is no major shortcut to peeling and prepping fresh garlic quickly. It's just something that takes time. But because garlic is such an important building block of flavor, it wouldn't be counterproductive to take a moment to focus on building that block. So, maybe give yourself a morning where you set a goal of peeling, slicing, or mincing a few heads of garlic. Once you hit the goal, transfer the prepped garlic to an airtight container and fridge it. Then, when you come home, it's ready to go just like any other pantry item, ready for use throughout the week.

That said, I do get it if your life's too busy or you just don't have the energy to set aside some garlic time. But don't let that stop you or keep you stagnant. In that case, do what you can. Use as much garlic as you have time to prepare, or pick up peeled cloves or jarred or frozen minced garlic from the market. No one's coming to your door if you go this way.

But if you do go this way, stop a moment. And taste.

Obviously, if you use less garlic than what I call for, the garlic flavors won't be as pronounced. If you use garlic that's been pre-peeled or pre-minced, the garlic flavor generally will be more muted than vibrant, one dimensional instead of three. Sometimes jarred or frozen minced garlic has a tinny or metallic flavor from the processing, or its flavor is affected by added salt or chemical preservatives.

So if you use fewer cloves than what's in the recipe, or you use pre-packed garlic, it may make sense to go off-script and pump up the volume on the other ingredients: Add more chiles or other aromatics, or throw in extra handfuls of herbs. Make the dish pop with lemon juice or another acid. The final result will taste and look different from what I have on the page. That's fine! That's what *The Choi of Cooking* is all about. It'll still be good. And it'll be you.

SCALLIONS

You can never have too many bunches in the fridge. Unless otherwise instructed, use the whole scallion, both the green and white parts.

LEMONGRASS

To prepare lemongrass for cooking, you'll need to first peel off the thicker, dryer leaves on the outside of the stalk until you get to the tender part inside. Then, trim the root and cut off the woodier part of the top. If you want, wash and save those parts and simmer them in some water with other vegetables, including their trimmings and scraps, to make a vegetable broth, or add it to a pot of stock to infuse it with flavor. Otherwise, toss in your compost bin or trash.

Depending on the dish, I'll either smash or mince the lemongrass. To smash, lay the prepped lemongrass on a cutting board, grab a pestle or a rolling pin or something pretty heavy, and bash the stalk a few times. To mince, first smash the lemongrass, then slice the stalk very finely with a sharp knife. You also can pick up a bag of frozen minced lemongrass from an Asian market; it's great to keep in your freezer for those times you don't have any fresh stalks, or it's a sweatpants day and you want to save a little time.

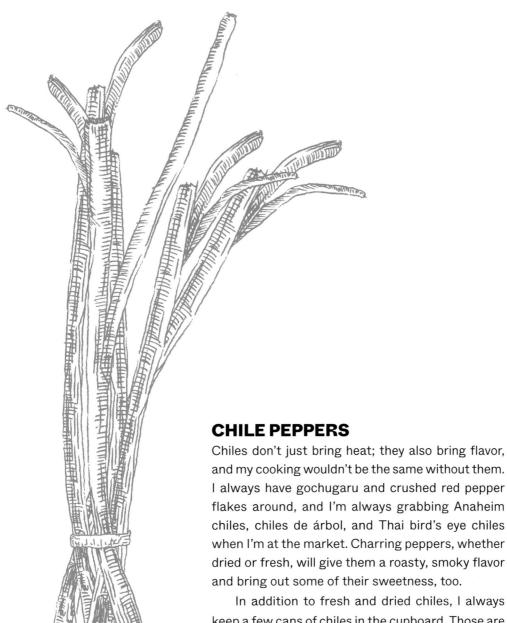

CHILE PEPPERS

Chiles don't just bring heat; they also bring flavor, and my cooking wouldn't be the same without them. I always have gochugaru and crushed red pepper flakes around, and I'm always grabbing Anaheim chiles, chiles de árbol, and Thai bird's eye chiles when I'm at the market. Charring peppers, whether dried or fresh, will give them a roasty, smoky flavor and bring out some of their sweetness, too.

In addition to fresh and dried chiles, I always keep a few cans of chiles in the cupboard. Those are great in burritos and in rice bowls.

Herb Garden

General rules of thumb: Dried herbs are good for rubs, roasts, and soups. Fresh herbs are always best for vinaigrettes and sauces. A handful of fresh herbs dropped into a dish right before serving will almost always bring something lively to the party, plus they add great pops of color.

In this book, I sometimes use dried herbs like oregano, but most of the herbs I use are fresh. And of those, the ones I reach for time and time again are cilantro, Italian basil, flat-leaf parsley, plus the following herbs that may need a little extra legwork to source depending on where you are:

THAI BASIL

This is more pungent and stronger in its licorice flavor than Italian basil. You can find it at many Asian markets, but if you can't source it, you can swap it out for Italian basil.

RAU RĂM

Sometimes called Vietnamese coriander or hot mint, this is a grassy, peppery herb with long, narrow leaves. Southeast Asian markets are a reliable source for rau răm, and many Asian markets carry it in their produce sections, too. If it's not available, you can sub in mint or lemon verbena.

PERILLA LEAF

A grassy herb with large leaves, you can find this at Korean and some Asian markets. It's also known as sesame leaf, although it's actually part of the mint family. Swap it out for shiso leaves or mint.

In the **Cupboard,**
on the **Counter,**
in the **Fridge**

BLACK PEPPER

Go with freshly grinding your own pepper if you can.

CHEESE

Cheddar in blocks or shredded and Parmesan (or Parmigiano-Reggiano) in wedges or grated. Use whatever form works for you, but have them both.

CITRUS

Lemons, limes, oranges, and yuzu all add bursts of acidity, brightness, flavor. They can transform a dish in an instant. Depending on where you are, you can find yuzu at your farmers' market or Japanese and specialty markets when it's in season, or use bottled yuzu juice.

FROZEN FRUIT AND VEGETABLES

Frozen fruit and vegetables have a place in our kitchen, especially for those times when you don't want to, or can't, get to the market. Frozen fruit is great for smoothies (page 49); and frozen corn, peas, broccoli, and spinach are just good basics to have on hand to throw into soups or rice or noodle bowls.

GOCHUJANG

You can get a tub and it'll keep in your fridge forever and you will never have to worry about not having enough to make a marinade or a dip or a stew. These days, stores sell gochujang in little tubes, too, so if you need it in a travel-friendly size, grab one of those.

GRAINS

Rice and noodles—all kinds of noodles, spaghetti, rice noodles, somen, udon—are everyday staples.

MSG

A little MSG to add a little extra never hurts.

NUTS

Nuts are great on their own, but you can take their natural flavors up a notch by toasting them. We'll do that a few times throughout the book, but toasting isn't just for cooking: Toast nuts for snacking, too. Just add the nuts to a pan over low heat for a few minutes, shaking the pan often to toast them evenly. Cool them before storing.

OILS

EXTRA-VIRGIN OLIVE OIL: You don't need anything fancy—just something you like and can afford. Olive oil is good for nearly everything, from cooking to making dressings to drizzling on at the last minute right before serving. But if you don't want to bring the olive flavor into your dish, go for a more neutral oil (see below).

NEUTRAL OIL WITH A HIGH SMOKE POINT: This would be oils like vegetable, corn, safflower, and grapeseed. These oils don't have a ton of flavor on their own and have high smoke points, which makes them good oils for frying.

TOASTED (OR ROASTED) SESAME OIL: Always toasted or roasted, never untoasted or unroasted. Use it sometimes for cooking, often in marinades, sauces, and dressings, and to finish a dish before serving. A little goes a long way.

SALT

I use Diamond Crystal kosher salt for cooking, which contains a lot less sodium per teaspoon than other brands of kosher salt like Morton. Diamond Crystal is available at many major supermarkets, and you can find it online. I'll call it out when I'm cooking with it, so if you're not using Diamond Crystal, start with half as much as I call for in the recipe, then taste taste taste as you're cooking and adjust the salt as needed.

Before serving, I sometimes use flaky sea salt to finish.

SAUCES

These little jars and bottles bring a ton of flavor to your dishes. I always have:

- Chili oil
- Chili garlic sauce or sambal oelek
- Fish sauce
- Hot sauce, at least one
- Oyster sauce
- Soy sauce
- Sriracha

TOASTED SESAME SEEDS

Like the oil, you'll see these labeled as toasted or roasted at the market. Good for their nutty flavor, good as a garnish.

A Quick Note About Cooking with

TOASTED SESAME OIL

The conventional rule about toasted sesame oil is that you can use it in a salad dressing, in a marinade or a dip, to finish a dish. The rule also says you definitely can't use it to sauté or stir-fry, because at medium and high temperatures, the oil will smoke and become bitter and make everything in the pan smoky and bitter, too. And those are bad flavors you want to avoid. So, according to the "rule," you should cook with a neutral oil.

I'm not sure when that rule became the rule, but it's not right. It's not that black and white.

Bitterness and smokiness aren't automatically bad. In some dishes, I don't want to avoid the bitterness and smokiness— I want to run right toward them, because I'm looking for the oil to go from toasty to smoky with an edge of bitter the same way some prize the charred ends of the brisket at the BBQ pit, or love the burnt parts of toast. This is the way I've been cooking for over twenty years. It's defined my flavor point and become part of my style, like the holes in my jeans. But, hey, if you try it and don't vibe with it, you don't have to cook with it like I do. In recipes where I cook with it, just swap out the toasted sesame oil for whatever neutral oil you do like.

TOFU

As I say in the tofu chapter (page 112), tofu (along with eggs) are the real MVPs in the kitchen. Tofu can be a snack or side on its own with just a little Soy-Ginger Sauce (page 244), it can play support in a breakfast burrito (page 118), it can be the main filling in a soup (page 142). Keep both soft and firm tofu in your fridge; you'll find ways to use them.

VINEGARS

Vinegars bring acid to your dish. There's a ton of different types of vinegars out there, from white wine to sherry to apple cider to balsamic, and they're all great to play with, especially when you're making your own vinaigrette (page 108). The vinegars I use the most in this book are rice, red wine, champagne, and balsamic; so if you're just starting to build out your pantry, you might want to start there and add to it as you cook more and use more. Note that rice vinegar sometimes comes seasoned; always get the unseasoned version for recipes in this book.

Equipment

You probably have everything you need to make most of the dishes in this book: measuring spoons, baking sheets, racks, whisks, big bowls to mix stuff in. I just want to call out a few things that I use a lot in here:

BLENDER

Sauces, marinades, milkshakes, dressings, frijoles: all blended. Being able to make a complex sauce from a dozen ingredients with a touch of a button will make it that much easier to get cooking.

There are a few recipes where a blender is super important, because it'll give you a sauce or a dressing that's totally combined, meaning the fats and vinegars and everything else are in full bear-hug mode. Blending emulsifies the ingredients in a way that you can't really do by hand; if you try whisking, for example, no matter how hard you whisk those ingredients, it won't be quite the same: The color will be a little duller, the texture a little thinner, the flavors a little flatter.

MICROPLANE

For zesting fruit and grating ginger, you can't beat it. Microplanes come in a few different sizes and grades of coarseness. If you get only one, I'd grab the classic rasp-style grater.

A FEW POTS AND SKILLETS

A cast-iron skillet is awesome for anything where you want to keep the heat constant, like frying. A Dutch oven and a large stockpot are both good for the soups and braises we'll make.

ON BLENDERS VS. FOOD PROCESSORS

For many of my recipes, I'm pretty specific about whether you should use a blender or a food processor to blend, puree, or combine certain ingredients. That's because which one you use when can make a difference. Think of it as the difference between making a smoothie in a blender and making one in a food processor: In a blender, your smoothie is going to be exactly that. Smooth. Unified. In a food processor, your smoothie will be a little chunkier, more like a mixture and less like a full integration of all the ingredients. It's the same for many sauces. A processor is great for many other things—pâtés, mousselines—but, the motor and blades on the blender are that much more effective at aerating and emulsifying. That's what I love about blenders, and that's why blenders are such a big part of my style of cooking: It's a smooth operator. And blending will get you a velvety ribbon that you just can't achieve with a food processor.

But, all that said, if you don't have the appliance I call for in a recipe, don't let that stop you. Use what you have, do it up, and make the recipe. Just know it'll be different. And if you have both appliances and want to experiment, try blending parts of some recipes and processing the rest. You'll see and taste what I mean.

STORAGE STUFF

Jars, food-grade plastic wrap, resealable food storage bags, deli and other containers that you saved and cleaned from last week's takeout to store leftovers. Because you will have leftovers.

TASTING SPOONS

Depending where you are in your cooking journey, it might be helpful to bring out a few spoons and keep them within an arm's reach. You want to constantly taste as you cook, to check on the seasoning, to adjust the flavors. If you haven't gotten into the practice of tasting all the time yet, then having the spoons nearby as a visual reminder is a small thing that will have a big impact.

This is the biggest chapter in this book, and that's intentional. Vegetables are a huge part of my cooking. So, if you love vegetables, this chapter is definitely for you. You will love vegetables even more.

And if you hate vegetables? This chapter is definitely for you. You will start to like vegetables a little more. Maybe you will even start to love them. I got you.

I think too often we don't treat vegetables with the respect they deserve. Many of us have grown up thinking vegetables are obligations, chores, a bad opening act you gotta sit through to get to the main protein or the dessert. So, they end up as afterthoughts. But it shouldn't be this way. Even when the vegetables are side dishes, they don't have to be side pieces. With some care, attention, and tons of flavor, they *can* steal the show. When that happens, I promise you'll want to dig into the vegetables as much as you want to dig into the big protein on the table.

So what I've got for you here are ways you can eat more vegetables without even realizing you're eating more vegetables. There will be vegetables you turn into refreshing pickles or kimchi. Vegetables you will eat raw because they're just the transport for the delicious dipping sauce. Vegetables that are grilled, roasted, sautéed, or braised and cooked with plenty of spices and acids to really make them pop.

Good *for* you, good *to* you, it's gonna be all good.

Eat these up. You'll officially be a veg head.

Drink Up

You can eat your vegetables and fruits, and you can drink your vegetables and fruits. So, I've got three drinks for you here: a smoothie, an agua fresca, and a green juice. The smoothie's in here because I love smoothies, and it's a great way to use fruit to satisfy your sweet cravings.

The juices are in here because I wanted to take this chance to simplify them a bit. What I mean is, the idea of juicing can be so complicated. For some, it means frozen orange juice concentrate out of a cardboard tube. For others, it's the greener-than-green drink you pick up while you're getting your groceries at the most expensive market in town. Meanwhile, the marketing for freshly pressed juices sells a lifestyle that you may or may not connect to, or can afford. But there's a bridge between those two worlds that we can build. That's what I hope those juices will be for you: planks on that bridge, juices that you'll want to make and drink whether you're used to drinking AriZona Iced Tea all day or whether you haven't touched a soda in over a decade.

AGUA FRESCA

48

Agua Fresca

MAKES 4 CUPS

Aguas frescas are to Los Angeles what coffee is to Seattle: It runs through the city's veins. When I was a kid, all the fruit juices around me were pressed fresh, whether it was my mom squeezing a bag of oranges or grapefruit into a glass before or after school, or the lady near the bus stop making aguas frescas using strawberries or tamarind and some lime juice. When you're at home, it's one of the easiest things you can make for yourself. And that's what this recipe is: a pretty straightforward pineapple agua fresca. It's a great place to start if you've never juiced anything before, and if you have, hopefully this adds to your repertoire. Like most aguas frescas, I add some lime and a sweetener (an agave-based simple syrup to limit the refined sugars I'm adding to my day); use the amounts I use as a guideline, but also keep in mind that the fruit's acidity and sweetness will change up depending on the season and where you get it from. So, before adding any sweetener, taste the fruit first to get a sense of how it tastes on its own. You may prefer to slowly add the simple syrup and lime juice to the blender and keep tasting until it's balanced the way you like it.

¼ cup hot water

¼ cup agave syrup

1½ cups cold water

4 cups diced pineapple

Juice of 1 lime

½ cup ice, plus another scoop for serving

Get In Where You Fit In

Really, fit in here with whatever you have. This agua fresca is also super refreshing with watermelon or any other type of melon. It's also great with berries or super-ripe mango; you can even make it with some crisp vegetables like jicama, or swap out the water for coconut water if that's your thing. And add herbs like mint or basil if you happen to have any extra in your crisper drawer.

1. In a mug or bowl, combine the hot water and agave syrup to make a simple syrup. Stir until the agave has completely dissolved.

2. Pour the cold water into a blender and add the pineapple, about half of the lime juice, 6 tablespoons of the agave simple syrup, and the ice. Puree until smooth, then taste. Add more lime juice if you want, or simple syrup to further sweeten. Once it's where you like it, strain the agua fresca, add some more ice, and drink up!

Smooth Operator

SERVES 4 TO 6

We all should be drinking more smoothies. They're easy to make, packed with fruit, and can be made in an infinite number of ways based on what you have. So think of this recipe as a base for your own custom smoothie. I use frozen berries, but use up whatever fruit you have in your freezer or on the counter. I like my smoothies to be thick 'n' creamy like a milkshake, but add a little more milk if you like them a little thinner. This recipe can easily be halved if you want just enough for yourself and a friend.

3 cups yogurt (any type)

3 cups frozen berries

1 cup almond milk

1 cup apple juice, orange juice, or açai juice

1 cup ice

1 banana

Juice of ½ lemon

2 tablespoons fresh mint

Salt

1 tablespoon agave syrup dissolved in 1 tablespoon hot water, or 2 tablespoons sugar (optional)

In a blender, combine the yogurt, berries, milk, juice, ice, banana, lemon juice, mint, and a pinch of salt. Puree until smooth, thick, and creamy. Taste. If you want it a little sweeter, add the diluted agave syrup or sugar to taste, pulsing once or twice to incorporate. Pour into glasses and serve.

Get In Where You Fit In

A few ideas for your custom smoothie: Experiment with different fruits, especially whatever's in season. I use mint here, but try different herbs: basil, cilantro, thyme. Or try adding chia seeds, ground turmeric, or grated fresh ginger.

Green Juice

MAKES 2½ CUPS

Odwalla and Naked Juice. Those were my first interactions with green juice, if you can call running away an interaction. Unlike Agua Fresca (page 48), I had zero context for green juice. A juicer was not a piece of equipment my family owned, or even knew existed. I understood the vegetables on their own: kale, spinach, celery, cucumber, ginger. Yeah. All those things I ate at home . . . but not usually at the same time, and not in liquid form. Meanwhile, all the marketing for green juice and the healthy lifestyle it promised to give you was clearly not aimed at people like us. The whole green juice thing just felt overwhelming, super daunting, and absolutely not something I wanted to try. I'll stick with my sodas, thanks.

When I did finally decide to try a green juice, I tried it from a place that did it fresh. And I was blown away. It was so good! And, honestly, it made me a little mad about all the life choices I'd made, or that were made for me, that made green juice so inaccessible to my part of LA, and to my friends. This green juice is me approaching you with something that I once thought was totally unapproachable. Use a juicer if you have one. If you don't, you can do this in a blender, too; have a sieve handy.

1 cucumber, quartered

1 green apple, cored and quartered

1 kiwi, quartered

1 lime, quartered or halved

½ lemon

2 cups loosely packed spinach

2 cups loosely packed baby kale

1½ cups sliced celery

¼ cup tightly packed fresh mint

¼ cup tightly packed fresh basil

¼ cup tightly packed fresh parsley

2½-inch piece fresh ginger

Place the cucumber, apple, kiwi, lime, lemon, spinach, baby kale, celery, mint, basil, parsley, and ginger into a juicer and juice. If using a blender, blend it all, then strain. Either way, give it a good stir, pour into glasses, and be green.

Get In Where You Fit In

Like aguas frescas, you can remix this with stuff you have in your fridge. Try adding carrots, or different herbs, or throw in a pinch of a spice like turmeric.

QUICKLES

Before I became a chef, pickles packed in jars were a big mystery to me. I thought they were born there, surrounded by glass. Then I grew up a little bit and learned those pickles are just vegetables! And that's when the stories started coming. It seemed like every sandwich I ate came with a mystical narrative about the pickle on the side, the origin story about its brine and its journey from raw to pickled. But to actually make a pickle, it's pretty easy! Anyone can make one, especially quick pickles like this one, where the vegetables turn into pickles after a few hours in a hot brine bath. You can use this brine to pickle any vegetable, but if you need a few ideas, start with okra, carrots, cabbage, red onions, and cucumbers and see how that goes. Hopefully this recipe will help you understand that pickles are magical, not mystical, things.

Get In Where You Fit In

Once you feel ready, this recipe can open a floodgate of flavor possibilities with the addition of aromatics and spices. You can make it spicy by adding chiles, for example, or make it a little sweeter with some pureed fruit. Or more savory with some soy sauce, and more punchy with herb stems or sprigs and spices like cumin seeds.

MAKES ABOUT 1 QUART

2 to 4 cups of whatever vegetables you want, cut any way you want

1½ cups rice vinegar

1 tablespoon minced garlic

2 teaspoons chopped fresh dill

1 tablespoon Diamond Crystal kosher salt

1 tablespoon sugar

1 bay leaf

1 tablespoon mustard seeds

1 teaspoon coriander seeds

1 teaspoon fennel seeds

1 teaspoon crushed red pepper flakes

1. Place the vegetables in a 1-quart jar (or split them among a few smaller jars or containers with lids).

2. In a medium pot, combine the vinegar, 1½ cups water, the garlic, dill, salt, sugar, bay leaf, mustard seeds, coriander seeds, fennel seeds, and pepper flakes. Bring it to a boil, then immediately pour over the vegetables. Make sure the vegetables are submerged in the brine so they'll pickle right.

3. Cool, uncovered, at room temperature. Cover and refrigerate. Once they've sat for a few hours, the pickles are ready. Keep in the fridge for up to 2 weeks.

WATERM

If you're used to only vegetable kimchis, trust me here: Bringing the savory element of kimchi to the sweetness of watermelon is a revelation. Don't stop there, though. Use this recipe to "kimchi" other fruits like melon, cantaloupe, papaya, mango, even oranges and put them all together in a fruit cup for a fun snack any time of the day.

SERVES 2 AS A SNACK

½ cup Kimchi Paste (page 255)

1½ pounds watermelon, cut into big chunks (about 4 cups)

Flaky sea salt and freshly ground black pepper

Lime wedges (optional)

Toasted sesame seeds (optional)

In a large bowl, combine the kimchi paste and ¼ cup water and stir to thin out the paste. Add the watermelon and toss to coat. Finish with salt and black pepper to taste. If desired, serve with lime wedges and shake the sesame seeds all over. It's best enjoyed immediately.

MELON KIMCHI

YAY,
CRUDITÉS

Crudités platters with sad baby carrots, cherry tomatoes, cucumbers, and a ranch dressing—that's what elementary and high school events are all about, right? There's gotta be a better way to eat crudités. I mean, *crudités* is just a fancy word for raw, crunchy vegetables with a dip. . . . And if you make a good dip, it can be a very effective way to eat more vegetables.

Raw Platter

SERVES 4 OR MORE

Raw Platter
(any or all of these):

2 tomatoes (any type), cut into wedges

2 Belgian endives, leaves separated

1 cucumber, unpeeled and cut into sticks
or spears

1 large carrot, cut into sticks

1 head radicchio, leaves separated

1 green (unripe) papaya, peeled
and cut into spears

1 green (unripe) mango, peeled
and cut into spears

1 head Little Gem lettuce,
leaves separated

½ head green cabbage, leaves separated

Dip
(choose one, choose two,
or do it up and choose 'em all!):

Roasted Eggplant and Tomato Dip
(page 58)

Korean Ssamjang Dip
(page 59)

Farmers' Market Pesto
(page 245)

Lemon Ranch Dressing
(page 106)

Old School Green Goddess
(page 105)

Prep all the vegetables and arrange on a platter. Place the dip
in a few bowls and set near the sliced veggies.

Roasted Eggplant and Tomato Dip

MAKES 2 CUPS

This dip for crudités is inspired by the flavors of Laotian dips, which are made using a huge variety of ingredients, from fish paste to shellfish to minced pork to vegetables. My version uses roasted vegetables as the base and includes some Chinese dark soy sauce to give it all a little bit of sweetness, depth, funkiness, and viscosity. Take this to your kid's next school performance and breathe fire!!

5 Thai eggplants or 1 large American eggplant, unpeeled, quartered

2 tomatoes (any kind), halved

Extra-virgin olive oil

Salt and freshly ground black pepper

Juice of 2 limes

1 cup chopped fresh cilantro

2 tablespoons minced Thai bird's eye or serrano chiles

2 tablespoons fish sauce

2 tablespoons Chinese dark soy sauce

1 tablespoon minced garlic

1 tablespoon minced shallots

1 tablespoon minced fresh ginger or galangal

Sugar (optional)

1. Preheat the oven to 400°F.

2. In a roasting pan or on a baking sheet, coat the eggplants and tomatoes in oil and season with salt and pepper. Roast until the vegetables are charred and soft, about 45 minutes.

3. Discard the peel from the eggplant if it's especially thick. Place the eggplant and tomatoes, along with their juicy juices, in a blender and puree until smooth. Add the lime juice, cilantro, chiles, fish sauce, soy sauce, garlic, shallots, and ginger and blend. Taste and adjust seasoning if necessary. If you want a little extra sweetness, add a pinch of sugar and puree again briefly, then serve with the raw veggies for dipping.

Korean Ssamjang Dip

MAKES ABOUT 2 CUPS

Here's another option for a crudités platter. This one is a quick Korean-style dip with gochujang and doenjang. It's also a great dip for my Steamed Pork Belly (page 218) or as part of any ssam platter (see Wrapper's Delight, page 220). If you can't find perilla or shiso leaves, you can use fresh mint instead, or omit them altogether.

1 jalapeño, minced

1 cup gochujang

1 cup doenjang or white miso paste

2 tablespoons minced perilla or shiso leaf

2 tablespoons rice vinegar

1 tablespoon minced garlic

1 tablespoon minced scallions

1 tablespoon toasted sesame oil

1 tablespoon soy sauce

Pinch of sugar (optional)

In a blender, combine the jalapeño, gochujang, doenjang, perilla leaf, vinegar, garlic, scallions, sesame oil, soy sauce, and 1 tablespoon water and blend until smooth. Taste and add a pinch of sugar if you'd like it a bit sweeter, then serve with raw veggies and take a dip.

AAA (THE TRIPLE A)

If you're feeling flat and out of gas, this is the sandwich you call up. This sandwich was actually inspired by some time I spent on a commune in upstate New York, where the diet was basically black bean soup and alfalfa sandwiches. And every time I had one of those sandwiches, I felt light and refreshed, as if I had just eaten a sandwich version of a green juice. So, yeah, everything about this sandwich screams healthy: the alfalfa sprouts, the avocado, the arugula. And I get it, if none of those things are your thing, maybe your instinct is to run away from it. But, let's not. Instead, let's try running toward it, toward these beautiful vegetables that have beautiful flavors if we let them shine.

MAKES 4 SANDWICHES

Unsalted butter, at room temperature

8 slices whole wheat bread

Your pick of spread: Mayonnaise, Farmers' Market Pesto (page 245), or Garlic Herbed Butter (page 244)

Big handful of alfalfa sprouts

Salt and freshly ground black pepper

1 avocado, sliced

Big handful of arugula

1 tomato (any variety as long it's ripe), sliced

1 cucumber, thinly sliced

1 small red onion, thinly sliced

4 to 8 slices cheddar cheese, depending on how much cheese you want

Handful of fresh basil leaves

1 bunch fresh cilantro, stems only

1 head romaine lettuce, leaves separated

A few spoonfuls of Dijon Balsamic Vinaigrette (page 102) or Broken Orange Vinaigrette (page 103)

1. Place a medium skillet or sauté pan over low heat. Butter both sides of the bread slices, place them in the pan, and toast until both sides are lightly browned. Take them out and place them on your work surface.

2. Spread your choice of spread on one side of 4 slices of bread, being sure to go edge to edge, corner to corner. Pile on the alfalfa sprouts, season them with salt and pepper, then add a few slices of avocado, some arugula, 2 or 3 tomato slices, cucumbers, red onions, 1 or 2 slices of cheddar, a few leaves of basil, cilantro stems, and romaine leaves. (If you want, you can season throughout, as you build the sandwich, but it's not super necessary.) Drizzle the vinaigrette over the leaves, close the sandwiches, and take a big bite.

STEP BY STEP

In the early days of Kogi BBQ, our food truck, I used to feed these young homies who mostly ate McDonald's every day. They tried our tacos and salsas, and I introduced them to an asparagus special we were running. They ate it all up. Then, the next week, they came back, walked right up to me—and asked how to cook asparagus. They still ate their Big Mac. But they learned how to cook asparagus.

This happened again with a bunch of our early skaters on a skate team we sponsored. They ate a burger with five-year-old cheddar cheese and slices of Parmesan with me for the first time when they were otherwise only eating processed shit. Now those skaters are real foodies, and a few have gone on to even become world-renowned chefs. We're talking about going from vapes and molly to organic grapes and cauli! Cot damn.

It's not obvious, but if you opened up the Kogi truck and took inventory, you'd see aged cheeses. You'd see that we're crammed full of fresh herbs and vegetables—but vegetables that move in silence like a G because they're pureed into salsas and sauces and marinades and garnishes. We just don't announce ourselves like that.

And that's just the way I cook, I guess. It revolves around vegetables, sometimes in obvious places like salads, but sometimes transformed into marinades and sauces. Or it's something like the Veggie on the Lo Mein Spaghetti (page 158) that at first looks like a gut bomb but is chock-full of vegetables.

This book is full of vegetables because that's the way I cook and eat. So, if you cook with vegetables all the time and are looking for some more bomb-ass veggie-centric food to make, my recipes are up your alley. If you don't, or if you're someone who calls Flamin' Hot Cheetos and Gatorade lunch and ends the day with fast food and diet sodas but you're thinking it's time to start eating more greens, I hope you can trust that this book is for you, too. Because my cooking philosophy is all about taking steps, not leaps, and moving away from extremes toward balance. It's about meeting you where you are, no matter where you are.

But you gotta take that first step. And the first step toward eating better than you do now is to know and control what you're putting in your pan and in your body. That means the first step is to cook. Full stop, that's it.

What you want to cook is up to you. I'll meet you where you are. Start with the burger, start with a stir-fry of chicken and green beans. Then, next time you make it, maybe wrap the burger in lettuce, or make the stir-fry with a little less chicken, a little more green beans. Work toward this the way you work a muscle: Like, you'd do some reps and then eventually go up ten pounds on the weights, right? Or run an extra block on your run? Same thing with adding veggies, trying new flavors. Then, next time, cook up another dish, this time one with a little more greens than you did before. Work the muscle. And each time you do this, each time you cook, you'll get better. Knowing what's behind the curtain gives you more control so you can make informed choices.

We've been brainwashed into thinking that healthy looks a certain way, like we all have to look like Adonis to be considered healthy. And we're very often judged on how we measure up, or don't measure up, to that standard. But healthy can look like a lot of different things. It can have different body shapes. It can mean moments of big salads and other moments of satisfied cravings. It doesn't have to be an either/ or thing. And there can be multiple roads and side doors to get there. So when you have a craving and need a release valve, I got you. The meals of our lives are a composite; no one dish defines how healthy or not we are. You can be on your journey toward wellness and satisfy your cravings. You can have both. I have both.

The way you cook and eat can be as pure as a monk's path or it could be a path that meanders even as it takes you forward. The key is to make that path a realistic one for you to take. So, make that burger, fry up some shrimp toast, build a Philly cheesesteak. Whatever you make, make it the best version it can be so you won't need to overindulge, then get back on the main road. As you progress, these recipes got your back.

And whichever path you take, we're going to arrive at the same spot, I promise you. Ingredients and techniques that were once foreign will become familiar. You'll go from instant ramen to rice noodles in a broth you made yourself. You'll go from skipping the salad to eating lettuces like a rabbit or an iguana, with nothing but an olive oil dressing hit with some lemon juice and seasoned with some salt and pepper that you shook up in a jar all on your own. And this shift in the way you cook might end up shifting the way you see yourself and others, too. If you eat a little more vegetables today than you did yesterday, and keep building on that, that's a win.

You got this. Flip through the book. Whatever looks good, cook that first. I'll meet you there.

THE FEEL GOOD
SANDWICH

I **wanted to give vegetarian sandwiches** a little love here, so I decided to take a bunch of vegetables I like—zucchini, eggplant, and mushrooms—and combine them into a super sandwich that will make you feel good all over. What you get from this sandwich is what you put in, so take the time to slice the veggies nicely and then grill them, bit by bit, so you end up with layers and layers of flavor. If you don't have a grill or want to make this indoors, slice the vegetables and either cook them in a skillet, ideally a cast-iron skillet, or place them on a sheet pan and roast them in a 350°F oven, checking on them frequently since they'll finish roasting at different times.

MAKES 4 SANDWICHES

1 zucchini

1 eggplant

2 portobello mushroom caps

½ head cabbage

1 red onion

1 head radicchio, leaves separated

Salt and freshly ground black pepper

Extra-virgin olive oil

Unsalted butter, at room temperature

8 slices seeded sandwich bread

2 ounces goat cheese

4 slices provolone cheese

Your pick of spread: Mayonnaise, Farmers' Market Pesto (page 245), or Garlic Herbed Butter (page 244)

2 avocados, sliced

2 cups loosely packed fresh basil leaves

1 lemon, halved

Flaky sea salt

Sherry vinegar

1. Preheat a grill to medium.

2. Slice the zucchini and eggplant lengthwise into slabs. Slice the mushrooms and cabbage, and slice the onion into rings. Slice all of these as thick or thin as you want, just keeping in mind that you'll be layering them into a fat stack for a sandwich. You'll want to be able to take a bite.

3. Keeping the vegetables separate so they'll be easier to organize on the grill, season the zucchini, eggplant, portobellos, cabbage, onion, and radicchio leaves with a generous pinch of salt and pepper. Coat them with some olive oil.

4. When the grill is nice and hot, start grilling the zucchini, eggplant, mushrooms, cabbage, and onions. How long this will take will depend on how thickly or thinly you sliced your vegetables, but generally, you want to get a nice char on each side and for them to warm through and their insides to become soft and velvety, so figure a few minutes per side for each. Add the radicchio leaves and grill just long enough for the leaves to char and wilt a bit, 1 minute max per side.

5. While the vegetables grill, butter both sides of all the bread slices and place them on the grill, too, and toast on both sides.

6. To assemble the sandwiches, spread the goat cheese on 4 slices of the bread.

7. Slather the remaining 4 slices of bread corner to corner with your pick of spread: the mayo or the pesto, or the butter. Pile on the zucchini, eggplant, mushrooms, provolone, cabbage, onions, radicchio, avocado slices, and a handful of basil leaves. Remove the seeds from the lemon and squeeze it over the basil, then add a bit of flaky sea salt, a splash of olive oil, and little sherry vinegar on top.

8. Smash the two sides together and you got a sandwich.

Calabrian Chile

BROCCOLI RABE

Broccoli rabe with caramelized garlic, lemon, basil, and a warm, fruity chile paste out of southern Italy: Yeah, there's nothing in here that seems distinctly Asian, but somehow this comes out like something you'd want to have alongside egg drop soup and a bowl of rice. It has a lot to do, I think, with what happens when you have first- and second-generation immigrant kids growing up on American soil. We just end up building things different, and this side is built different. It channels the sort of wood-fire-kissed sides you would get at a classic Italian trattoria, but it's cooked more like a stir-fry, with everything thrown in a wok and blistered at high heat. Eat it with pasta, eat It with rice. When you're shopping, note that some markets may have broccoli rabe labeled on the bin under its Italian name, rapini.

SERVES 4

2 bunches broccoli rabe

5 tablespoons extra-virgin olive oil, plus more as needed

2 cups whole garlic (60 to 70 cloves), sliced

Salt and freshly ground black pepper

2 tablespoons Calabrian chile paste (see Get In Where You Fit In)

Juice of 1 lemon

1 cup chopped fresh basil

Fennel pollen (see Get In Where You Fit In)

Dried oregano

Handful of fresh basil leaves, for garnish

1. Slice off the thicker woodier base of the rabe's stems and discard or compost. Cut the broccoli rabe in half or in thirds, depending on how large the bunches are. For looks, cut them on a bias.

2. Place a large wok or pan over high heat and add the olive oil. When the oil begins to shimmer, add the garlic slices and sauté until they're aromatic, 3 to 4 minutes. Add the broccoli rabe and give the pan a good toss so the garlic lands on top of the broccoli. Season with salt and pepper and toss again. If necessary, add a little more olive oil to keep things moving.

3. Add 2 tablespoons water and keep tossing the broccoli and garlic together until the broccoli is just al dente, 4 to 5 minutes. Add the chile paste and lemon juice and sauté for 1 to 2 more minutes to incorporate and mellow out the heat. Add the chopped basil, a pinch of fennel pollen, and a very light sprinkle of oregano. Taste and adjust the seasoning.

4. Transfer the broccoli rabe to a large plate or platter, splash a bit of olive oil on top, and shower it all with the basil leaves. Serve.

Get In Where You Fit In

- Italian and specialty markets sell Calabrian chile paste; if you can't get it, pick up a jar of Calabrian chiles in oil and mash it to form a paste.

- The pinch of fennel pollen right at the end gives the rabe a citrusy, licorice-y flavor. You can use ground fennel instead; use 2 pinches of it instead of one, or add it to taste.

- This recipe also will work with a ton of other vegetables, like broccolini, cauliflower, eggplant, zucchini or any other summer squash, green beans, or snap peas.

STIR-FRIED
PEA SHOOTS
WITH GARLIC AND CHILES

This dish was raised by wolves. When I was a kid, I was constantly being told by my elders I was eating stuff the "wrong" way. I wasn't supposed to eat rice with soup, I wasn't supposed to add soy sauce or chili oil to the restaurant's already perfect platter of steamed or stir-fried vegetables. I didn't mean any disrespect; it was just the way I liked to eat. But *that's how dogs eat*, they'd say, and there would be all this classist shit wrapped up in that and left unsaid but felt. But you know? What if the dogs got it right? I'm grown up now, and I want to take all that passive-aggressive—and some straight-up aggressive—shit from back then and reprocess it back to you with love. That's this stir-fry. Stir-fried pea shoots is a dish I love to get when I can get it. Instead of adding the condiments I would add when the plate hits the table, I'm adding them right into the cook. As with most stir-fries, everything happens fast once the first ingredient hits the pan—the pea shoots especially will wilt the second they feel the wok's hot breath—so get everything prepped out before you turn on the heat. Once you make it, give it a taste and absolutely add anything else you want to add to it to make it your own. No judgment here. Who let the dogs out?

SERVES 4 TO 6

1 tablespoon toasted sesame oil

1 cup whole garlic cloves (30 to 40 cloves), sliced

1 cup sliced shallots

1 cup sliced yellow onions

1 cup minced scallions

16 ounces pea shoots

1 cup sliced Fresno chiles or jalapeños (7 to 10 chiles), plus more for garnish if you want

Salt and freshly ground black pepper

2 tablespoons chili oil

¼ cup soy sauce

Juice of 1 lime

¼ cup chopped unsalted roasted peanuts, for garnish

¼ cup store-bought fried garlic slivers, crispy fried onions, or onion strings (optional), for garnish

¼ cup chopped fresh cilantro, for garnish

1. Set a large pan or wok over high heat. Once hot, add the sesame oil, garlic, shallots, onions, and scallions. Sauté until they're aromatic and begin to turn translucent, about 3 minutes. Add the pea shoots and give it all a good stir. Add the chiles and season very lightly with salt and a good pinch of pepper. Quickly toss everything and add the chili oil, soy sauce, and lime juice. Give it one more quick toss to combine, then turn off the heat.

2. Plate it up and garnish with the peanuts, fried garlic (if using), cilantro, and additional chiles.

CHOICE WORDS: It seems like such a minor thing, I know, to add chili oil and soy sauce and lime juice to this stir-fry, but it's nothing like the more simply prepared versions I ate growing up. Don't get me wrong, I love those versions, too; I just always liked adding those little extra extras on top. And that sums up something I want to convey to you through this book: Cook whatever the fuck you want. Everything I put in this book is the result of a lifetime of experiences and cooking, and when I'm left to roam free, these are all the things I make. I can teach you technique and methods and basic foundations of flavor, but the big picture I hope you take home is that cooking can be an expression of you—your own tastes, your own point of view, you. Finding the strength to express it can be tough, but keep cooking and you'll build up the confidence, just like any other muscle.

Get In Where You Fit In

Instead of pea shoots, this stir-fry will also be great with daikon sprouts, morning glory (the stems and leaves), spinach, dandelion greens, chrysanthemum greens, mizuna, haricots verts, or baby kale.

Grilled Artichoke and Zucchini

with Lemon Ranch Dressing

This is my contribution to the outdoor summer barbecue. Vegetables sometimes have a hard time competing against the burgers and the steaks on the grill, so I want to give them an assist, a fighting chance to hold their own against the heavy proteins. I do that by charring the vegetables well on the grill and serving them with a really delicious ranch dressing made from scratch. I picked whole artichokes for the grill because I think artichokes are underrated. They are so delicious, but they take a minute to prepare so we just don't eat them as much as we should. I want to convince you that they're worth your time. And zucchini—well, zucchini are just great grilling vegetables, plain and simple. And even though this is for a BBQ, you can make this indoors any time of the year. Just sear and cook the artichokes and zucchini on the stove in a grill pan or skillet, or put them under the broiler for a few minutes.

SERVES A BBQ PARTY

6 artichokes

1 lemon, halved

6 zucchini

Extra-virgin olive oil

Salt and freshly ground black pepper

Lemon Ranch Dressing (page 106)

1. Snap off a layer or two of the outer leaves of the artichokes as they tend to be tougher. Slice off their stems and, using kitchen shears, cut off the spiky tips on each artichoke leaf. Cut the artichokes in half, from top to stem. Use a spoon to scoop out the fuzzy center (the choke). Discard the chokes, rub the cut sides of the artichokes with a lemon half and place them in water so they keep their color.

2. Fill a steamer or a pot with a steamer insert with 2 inches of water and bring the water to a boil. Place the artichoke halves cut-side down in the steamer and steam. Check the artichokes after 10 minutes: You'll know they're done when the leaves are tender and you can easily pierce the heart with a knife. Remove the cooked artichokes from the pot, drain in a colander, pat dry, and place them on a baking sheet.

3. Preheat a grill to high (or place a grill pan or skillet on the stove over high heat).

4. Slice the zucchini in half lengthwise and place them on the sheet with the artichokes. Coat the vegetables in oil and season with salt and pepper.

5. Oil the grates of the grill and place the artichokes and the zucchini cut-side down. Cook them till they're charred, about 10 minutes. Flip and cook for another 5 or so minutes. You're looking for the zucchini to soften, but they should still keep their shape.

6. Place the other half of the lemon, cut-side down, on the grill, too.

7. Just as the vegetables are about done, drizzle them lightly with olive oil for one final caramelization.

8. Place the artichokes and zucchini on a platter or large plate and squeeze the charred lemon over the vegetables. Spoon some of the lemon ranch dressing over the entire platter. Pass the rest of the dressing in a bowl.

Sweatpants Version + Get In Where You Fit In

If you don't have time to clean the artichokes, or you don't have artichokes, swap them out for any other type of squash, eggplant, or portobello mushrooms. Even lettuces, napa cabbage leaves, or radicchio can be grilled until charred and will be great with the dressing.

THE CHOI OF COOKING

HOT CHOW CHOW

To cook **Swiss chard,** I like to put it in a shallow pot and braise it slowly to give it time to break down and become tender. And in the time it takes to braise the thick leaves and thicker stems, I thought we could bring in some acid and heat to give the bunches a symphony of flavors—specifically, acid from some vinegar, and heat from a few dashes of Tabasco. All together, this braise ends up being a little bit like the chow chow relishes I had when I spent some time in Virginia and Georgia. This dish is an ode to that period. If you can, go with bunches of rainbow chard to give the dish some color and fun. Serve it with any simply prepared protein, like a steak or pork chops or that rotisserie chicken you picked up from the market.

Get In Where You Fit In

In addition to Swiss chard, this braise will work for any tough green like kale, collard greens, or kohlrabi leaves.

SERVES 4 TO 6

1 tablespoon extra-virgin olive oil

4 ounces pancetta, finely diced

1 cup whole garlic cloves (30 to 40 cloves), sliced

½ cup sliced shallots

Salt and freshly ground black pepper

2 to 3 pounds Swiss chard (4 to 5 bunches), roughly chopped

1 cup chicken stock

½ cup red wine vinegar

1½ tablespoons unsalted butter

¾ teaspoon chopped fresh rosemary

Tabasco sauce

1. Set a large shallow pot with a lid over medium-high heat and add the oil and pancetta. Cook, stirring, until the pancetta starts to crisp and its fat has rendered, 3 to 4 minutes.

2. Add the garlic and shallots and season with just a touch of salt (be careful here, as the pancetta already is salty) and a good bit of black pepper. Sauté the pancetta, garlic, and shallots until the garlic and shallots have softened and become aromatic, 2 to 3 minutes.

3. Add all of the chard and increase the heat to high. Using tongs, mix the chard with the other ingredients and cook until the leaves have wilted slightly, about 1 minute. Deglaze the pot by adding the stock and vinegar and switching to a wooden spoon to scrape up and release all the caramelized bits stuck to the bottom.

4. Taste, reseason if needed, then cover and drop the heat to low. Simmer the chard for 6 minutes. Uncover and add the butter, rosemary, and a splash of Tabasco. Stir, increase the heat to high, and cook, uncovered, just until the chard is tender and the liquid has reduced but is still viscous, 1 to 2 more minutes.

5. Place the chard on a large platter or in a bowl, spoon the liquid all over, and serve.

ROASTE

I hate carrots. I hate carrots, but they're good for you. I hate carrots, but they're good for you, so I have to almost trick myself into eating them by coming up with some way of cooking them so I would eat them. And I've cracked the riddle by layering the carrots with flavor every step of the way: roasting them till they're charred to bring out their natural sweetness, tossing them with tons of garlic, and, finally, smothering them with a bright, herby vinaigrette. If I could convince myself to cook and eat these carrots, you can, too.

SERVES 4 TO 6

3 pounds carrots, tops trimmed to 1 to 2 inches

½ bunch fresh thyme

20 whole garlic cloves, peeled

Salt and freshly ground black pepper

½ cup extra-virgin olive oil, or as much as you need to coat the carrots

½ cup Broken Orange Vinaigrette (page 103)

1. Preheat the oven to 400°F.

2. If your carrots are on the smaller or thinner side, leave them whole. Otherwise, slice them in half lengthwise. Place the carrots on a sheet pan.

3. Set aside a few sprigs of thyme, then add the rest of the bunch to the pan with the carrots, along with the garlic cloves and a good seasoning of salt and pepper. Coat the carrots with olive oil.

4. Arrange the carrots in a single layer and place in the oven. Roast until the carrots are shiny, wrinkly, charred, and caramelized, 45 minutes to 1 hour. They should be tender, but still have their shape, and the garlic should be soft.

5. To serve, smush the garlic cloves with a fork and gently toss them with the carrots. Transfer the vegetables to a platter, place the thyme sprigs you set aside earlier right on top, pour the vinaigrette all over, and serve.

Get In Where You Fit In

You can use this recipe with any vegetable you hate. For example, hate turnips, radishes, or parsnips? Use those. It's all about being willing to confront yourself and your burdens, using the experience to grow, and ultimately being open to changing your perspectives.

⊃ GARLIC CARROTS

with Broken Orange Vinaigrette

ROASTED BEETS WITH CHILI CRISP, CILANTRO, AND LIME

If you don't always have vegetables on the table with your meal, this recipe is for you. Everything about this is designed to make your day easy: You pop the beets into the oven to bring out their natural sweetness, and you make a quick savory sauce to complement the beets. That's it. These beets are great hot out of the oven or cold out of the fridge, so pack up the leftovers and they'll be ready for the next meal.

SERVES 4 TO 6

4 medium beets (any color), scrubbed and dried

Extra-virgin olive oil

Salt and freshly ground black pepper

Grated zest and juice of 2 limes

2 tablespoons chopped fresh thyme

2 tablespoons chopped fresh Thai basil

2 tablespoons chopped fresh cilantro

2 tablespoons minced lemongrass (see Lemongrass, page 34)

2 tablespoons chili crisp

2 tablespoons rice vinegar

1 tablespoon fish sauce

1. Preheat the oven to 400°F.

2. In a large roasting pan, smother the beets with olive oil and season with salt and pepper. Cover the pan with foil and roast until the beets are tender, about 1 hour 15 minutes, depending on the size of the beets.

3. While they're still hot, carefully peel the beets. Cut the peeled beets into big chunks.

4. In a large bowl, mix together the lime zest, lime juice, thyme, Thai basil, cilantro, lemongrass, chili crisp, vinegar, and fish sauce. Add the beets to the mixture and stir to combine. Serve.

Get In Where You Fit In

- This recipe also works with carrots, turnips, radishes, cauliflower, fennel, and rutabagas. You can even roast cabbage leaves and thick wedges of yellow onion. If you do choose a more delicate vegetable, check to see if they're charred and tender at 15 minutes.

- I use a bunch of different fresh herbs to really punch up the flavor, including Thai basil and lemongrass; if you can't find Thai basil, swap it out for Italian basil. And if you can't find lemongrass, try it with lemon verbena or ginger instead.

ROASTED CAULIFLOWER STEAKS

with Harissa and Garlic Herbed Butter

If you follow trends and shit, it seems like roasted cauliflower steaks cycle in and out of the zeitgeist. One day they're passé, the next, they're the thing to eat. That's a shame, because cauliflower steaks are *always* so delicious, and you don't need to do much more than roast them with harissa, paprika, and an herbed butter to give the cauliflower tons of flavor. Serve them up with a bowl of rice and you have an easy weeknight meal.

SERVES 4

2 large cauliflowers, any color of the rainbow

Extra-virgin olive oil

¾ to 1 cup harissa, to taste

Salt and freshly ground black pepper

Smoked paprika

Garlic Herbed Butter (page 244)

1. Preheat the oven to 375°F.

2. Slice the cauliflower into 1-inch steaks (see How to Slice a Cauliflower into Steaks below). Place the steaks on a sheet pan and coat each in olive oil. Smother them in harissa, then season with salt, pepper, and a few pinches of smoked paprika. Arrange the steaks in a single layer and roast until they're charred and tender enough that they can be pierced with a fork, about 20 minutes, flipping the steaks halfway through the roast.

3. Remove the cauliflower and add a pat or two of the garlic butter right on top of each steak. Return it to the oven for 5 minutes to caramelize, then remove.

4. Now, you can have some fun with this, especially if you aren't a chef but want to look like one: Place a steak slightly off-center on a large plate. Tilt the baking sheet to gather all the oils and juices from the roast and spoon some all over the steak. Add a knob of the garlic herbed butter on top, wipe the edges of the plate clean, sprinkle a little more paprika on top, and serve.

HOW TO SLICE A CAULIFLOWER INTO STEAKS
To slice a head of cauliflower into steaks, first trim away the large, thick green leaves around the base, then flip the cauliflower on its head so it's stem-side up. Cut the cauliflower in half through the stem. From there, slice each half into a 1-inch steak, trimming it as necessary. You'll end up with a bunch of florets that fall off as you cut; toss them into the pan and roast them, too, or save them for another use (they'll be great, for example, added to any of my soups, pages 132 to 149).

CARROT (PAN)CAKES

I **grew up on pancakes.** Not classic American ones with maple syrup, but jeon, savory Korean pancakes filled with chives or mung beans or potatoes with a side of soy sauce for dipping, eaten every time of the day as part of a meal or as a midnight snack. This recipe is sort of a hybrid of all of those savory pancakes, with mung beans, potatoes, chives, tempura batter mix (for a little extra crisp in the batter), and tons of vegetables folded in. You *can* make a bunch of these and place them pretty on a tray and bring them out to the table but, honestly, grabbing them right out of the pan as they're made is the best, and most fun, way to enjoy these. Note that the mung beans need to be soaked overnight before using, so plan accordingly. For the dip, you can make the one I have here, or use the Soy-Ginger Sauce (page 244) instead.

MAKES 6 TO 8 (PAN)CAKES

Dip
Rice vinegar
Soy sauce
Gochugaru
Sugar

Get In Where You Fit In

- Tempura batter mix helps give the pancakes a bit of crisp. In addition to Asian markets, you can find it in many major supermarket chains. If necessary, you can use pancake mix, preferably unsweetened, instead, or make your own mix by combining ½ cup all-purpose flour, ½ cup rice flour, a small pinch of salt, a pinch of baking powder, and a heavy pinch of cornstarch.

- Pureeing all the vegetables together into the batter will result in a pancake that has a very soft, almost custardy interior. If you prefer a firmer texture, blend everything but the scallions, zucchini, and carrots. Pour the batter into a large bowl and gently fold in the scallions, zucchini, and carrots and continue with the rest of the recipe.

1. *Make the dip:* Make as much as you need by stirring together equal amounts of vinegar and soy sauce along with a pinch of gochugaru and a pinch of sugar. Taste and adjust the flavor, then set it aside while you make the pancakes.

2. *Make the pancakes:* Peel the potato and cut it into large chunks, keeping the pieces submerged in a bowl of cold water to keep them crisp. Using the small holes on a box grater, finely grate the potatoes into a medium bowl. Add the grated potatoes to a blender along with the mung beans, their soaking liquid, scallions, zucchini, carrots, onion, tempura batter mix, chives, salt, a bit of pepper, and ¼ cup water (see Get In Where You Fit In). Puree until smooth, about 30 seconds.

3. Line a plate or sheet pan with paper towels and set it next to the stove. Place a nonstick griddle or large nonstick skillet over medium heat. Drizzle the cooking surface generously with oil. Once the oil begins to smoke, drop a spoonful of batter into the pan. You'll cook this mini pancake just to check the seasoning. Cook this tester pancake until it starts to brown and puff up a bit; you'll see a crust start to form around the edges and tiny

(Pan)Cakes

1 large russet potato

½ cup split yellow mung beans, soaked overnight in 1½ cups water (don't toss the soaking water)

2 scallions, thinly sliced, plus 1 thinly sliced scallion for garnish

2 zucchini, grated and squeezed dry

2 small carrots, shredded

½ medium yellow onion, roughly chopped

1 cup tempura batter mix (see Get In Where You Fit In)

½ cup thinly sliced fresh chives

1 teaspoon Diamond Crystal kosher salt, plus more to taste

Freshly ground black pepper

Vegetable oil or other neutral oil, for greasing the pan

bubbles dotting the surface of the pancake, 1 minute or so. Flip the pancake and cook the other side, 30 seconds to 1 minute. Taste the pancake and add more salt or pepper or both to the batter if it needs it.

4. After getting the seasoning to where you want it, ladle a heaping ½ cup of batter onto the griddle. You should hear the pancake sizzle as soon as it hits the pan. Spread the batter 4 to 5 inches in diameter. Cook until it's crisped around the edges and a bunch of bubbles bubble up on the surface, 3 to 4 minutes, then flip and cook the other side, 2 to 3 minutes. The pancakes should be crispy on the outside and soft (but cooked) on the inside, almost like a crème brûlée.

5. Serve it right out of the pan with the dipping sauce, or place the pancake on the paper towels to drain while you make the rest. Repeat with the remaining batter, re-oiling the griddle as necessary. Watch the heat, too, and adjust it up or down as necessary. The griddle should be hot enough that the pancakes brown and crisp up, but not so hot that they burn.

CRISPY MASHED POTATOES

THE CHOI OF COOKING

These potatoes are mashed and then crisped up in a cast-iron skillet . . . basically, the best part of mashed potatoes meets the best part of hash browns, with tons of flavor from chives, thyme, and garlic. This dish is a great family dish, a crowd-pleaser that slots in with almost any meal. It's also a go-to comfort dish for those times when a potato or strong carb craving hits; make this yourself and you'll not just satisfy that craving, but learn a cooking lesson you can take with you anywhere. Even if you don't cook very often, this is a really good recipe to try, because it's not too complicated; the biggest lesson here is patience, as the potatoes will need time to crisp up. Resist the temptation to rush the process, though, and you won't go wrong. You will need to flip the potatoes so both sides develop a sturdy crust. That may sound scary, but if you cook the potatoes in a small cast-iron skillet, it'll be easy-peasy.

Power Up

A few spoonfuls of these potatoes will go a long way. Balance them with lean proteins, like a rotisserie chicken from the market or a salmon fillet (page 192), and steamed or grilled vegetables like the Grilled Artichoke and Zucchini (page 70).

SERVES 4

1½ pounds Yukon Gold potatoes, peeled

Salt and freshly ground black pepper

½ cup minced fresh chives, plus more for garnish

4 tablespoons (½ stick) unsalted butter, at room temperature, plus more for the skillet

1 tablespoon chopped fresh thyme, plus more for garnish

1 tablespoon minced garlic

Extra-virgin olive oil

Lemon wedge, for squeezing

Ketchup, for serving

1. Place the potatoes in a medium or large pot and fill the pot with enough water to cover the potatoes by an inch or two. Set over high heat, add a generous pinch of salt, bring to a boil, and cook the potatoes until they're knife-tender, 15 to 20 minutes. Drain and set the potatoes aside to cool completely.

2. Once cooled, grate the potatoes into a large bowl. Season the potatoes with salt and pepper, then add the chives, 4 tablespoons butter, the thyme, and garlic. Gently mash and stir everything together to get a nice sludge. Don't be too aggressive, though. You want the potatoes to be light and fluffy.

3. In a 6- or 8-inch cast-iron skillet, heat 1 to 2 tablespoons of butter and enough oil to coat the bottom of the skillet over medium heat. When the oil starts to shimmer, add the potatoes and spread them into an even round with a thickness of 1½ to 2 inches. Leave the potatoes alone to crisp, 6 to 8 minutes.

4. Once the potatoes have developed a nice golden crust, place a large plate upside down over the pan and, with one hand on top of the plate and the other hand on the handle of the pan, flip so the potatoes land crust-side up on the plate. Set the pan back on the burner, add 1 to 2 tablespoons butter and a drizzle of oil, and slide the potatoes back into the pan to crisp the other side, 10 to 13 minutes.

5. Flip one more time onto the plate, then slide the potatoes back into the pan. Rewarm this side just for 1 to 2 minutes, then place it on the plate. Squeeze the wedge of lemon over the potatoes. Garnish with chives and thyme and serve with ketchup on the side.

BOMB-ASS FRIJOLES
WITH ROASTED POBLANOS

When I was a kid, our family moved a lot, all over Los Angeles. But wherever we ended up, I'd end up making friends with the neighborhood kids, and their mothers and grandmothers would pull me in and welcome me to their tables with frijoles and other warm meals. And so, refried beans became as much a part of my upbringing as Korean steamed eggs and pots of rice and instant ramen. This recipe is an ode to all the Latino and Chicano families who nurtured me and gave me such love back then. It's not an exact replica of what they fed me; it's more like a cover version in tribute, one that hits on that core memory and feelings of nostalgia while, I hope, adding something new. Eat them with everything, or fold them into a Bean and Cheese Burrito (page 86). A heads-up that the beans need at least 4 hours to soak before they're ready to cook.

SERVES 6 TO 8

1 pound dried pinto beans

2 California chiles (dried Anaheim chiles), or any other dried chile

Extra-virgin olive oil

1 medium yellow onion, minced, plus more for garnish

1 cup whole garlic cloves (30 to 40 cloves), chopped

Salt and freshly ground black pepper

3 plum tomatoes, chopped

2 tomatillos, husked, rinsed, and chopped

1 jalapeño, chopped

2 cups chopped fresh cilantro, plus more for garnish

2 cups canned chopped fire-roasted poblano peppers or green chiles (about two 7-ounce cans)

Juice of 1 lime, plus lime wedges for serving

4 tablespoons Tapatío or other hot sauce, or to taste

2 tablespoons dried oregano

1 teaspoon crushed red pepper flakes

2 tablespoons unsalted butter

Crumbled Cotija cheese, for garnish

1. Place the beans in a large bowl and add water to cover by at least 2 inches. Soak them overnight, or for at least 4 hours, then drain.

2. When you're ready to cook the beans, soak the dried chiles in a bowl of warm water to rehydrate, about 15 minutes. Drain and chop.

3. Meanwhile, in a 6-quart Dutch oven or soup pot, warm 2 tablespoons of olive oil over high heat. When it begins to shimmer, add the onion and garlic. Season with salt and pepper and sauté for 1 to 2 minutes, adding a little more oil if they're sticking to the pot. You're looking to caramelize these aromatics at this point, and to cook the rawness out of the garlic.

4. Add the tomatoes and tomatillos and sauté for another minute or two. Add the drained rehydrated chiles and the jalapeño and sauté for 1 minute. Add the beans and sauté for 1 to 2 minutes, just to toast them a little bit. Add 4 cups water and bring to a boil, then reduce the heat and simmer until the beans soften, about 1 hour.

5. Add the cilantro, canned poblanos, and lime juice and give it all a good stir. Transfer everything to a blender, working in batches if necessary so you don't overload your blender. Puree until smooth, then reseason with salt and pepper. Return the beans to the pot, set over medium heat, and stir in the hot sauce, oregano, and pepper flakes. Taste and adjust the seasoning, then add a swirl of olive oil. Cover and simmer the beans for about 20 minutes to reduce and thicken.

6. To finish, stir the butter into the pot of beans. Scoop spoonfuls into bowls or plates, garnish with minced onion, cilantro, and Cotija, and serve with the lime wedges and the bottle of hot sauce for the table.

BEAN AN
BURRI

When I was a kid and things were tight with my parents struggling to get by, bean and cheese burritos were a huge part of my life. I lived off of them again when I was in my late teens to mid-twenties and broke as fuck. All that's to say, I have a real love for bean and cheese burritos. This version is for those times when you have the craving, but can't make it out to your local taqueria or want to tuck into a homemade version. When it comes to actually making the burrito, I like to start building it right in a pan so everything is warmed up a bit before I slide it off onto a cutting board to roll it up. For the salsa, I combine pico de gallo with salsa roja to make a sort of soupy pico de gallo, but you can always keep them separate if you want.

MAKES 4 BURRITOS

½ cup Pico de Gallo (page 251)

¼ cup Salsa Roja (page 251)

Extra-virgin olive oil

4 (10- to 12-inch) flour tortillas

1 to 1½ cups Bomb-Ass Frijoles with Roasted Poblanos (page 84)

8 ounces shredded cheddar cheese

4 to 5 ounces canned diced green chiles

1. In a small bowl, mix the pico de gallo with the salsa roja and set aside.

2. In a large pan or griddle over low heat, add a kiss of olive oil and warm it up for about 15 seconds. Add a tortilla, bumpier-side down, and cook. Once it begins to blister and is toasted but still pliable, 30 to 45 seconds, flip.

3. Add the beans along the lower third of the tortilla (how much you add depends on the size of the tortilla; start with ¼ or ⅓ cup and see how that goes). Add a handful of cheese, a spoonful of the salsa mix, and some green chiles.

4. Carefully slide the whole thing to a cutting board or a large plate, tuck in the sides, and roll it all up. Make the remaining burritos the same way and serve.

Sweatpants Version

Instead of making the frijoles from scratch, you can use a can of refried beans from the market.

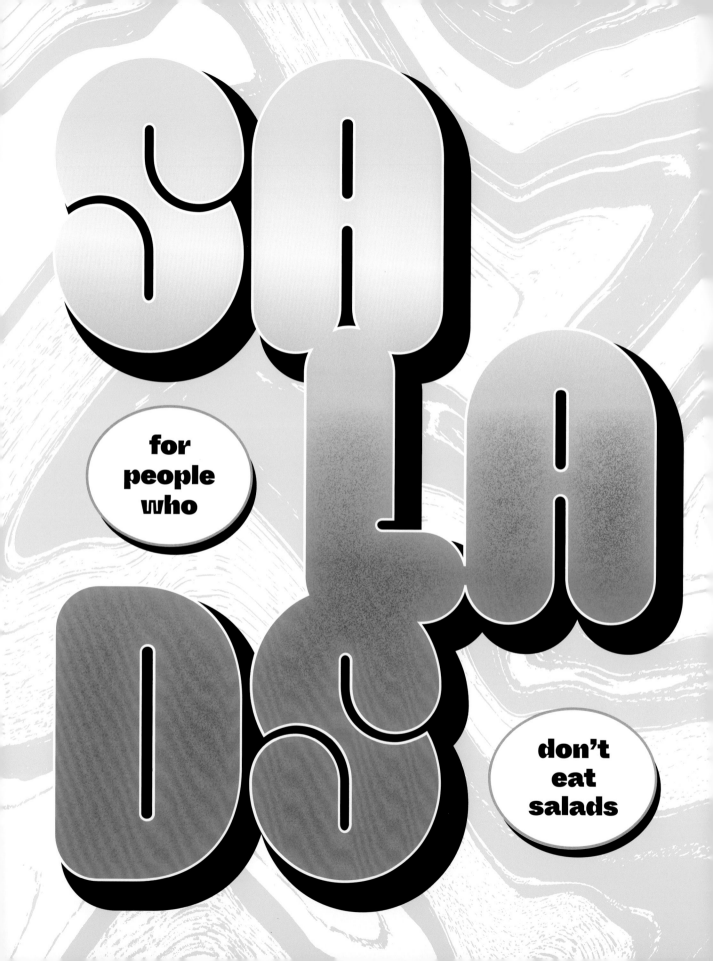

We can front all day about how healthy salads are, and how important it is to eat a big bowl of greens every day, but let's be honest: A lot of us aren't eating salads on a regular basis. I don't love salads either, so for me to want to eat, much less make, a salad, there has to be something interesting or exciting or different about it.

So this chapter is all about making salads that anyone will want to eat, including me. And to make salads that we all will want to eat, I'm dropping you into them the way Tarantino drops you into the diner with Pumpkin and Honey Bunny at the beginning of *Pulp Fiction*: right in the middle of something that feels familiar but unexpected and dramatic, something that grabs your attention. From making a vinaigrette that tastes like Orange Bang to a salad topped with potato chips, the salads in this chapter are designed to be accessible and fun and to break down walls about what salads can and can't be. I'll even show you how to make your own vinaigrette, so you'll always be able to outfit your greens with whatever you have in your kitchen. Most dressings will store well for a few days in the fridge, so make a good amount and it'll be that much easier to throw together another bowl of salad tomorrow.

BIG FUCKING SALAD

with Dijon Balsamic Vinaigrette

This is essentially a salad bar salad, what you make because you're at the salad bar staring at a bunch of little tongs and endless rows of lettuces, raw vegetables, fruit, nuts, croutons, bread crumbs, and every dressing ever made. It brings together a few things for me:

Memories of building salads leaf by leaf at Sizzler's and Wendy's salad bars when I was a kid.

The salad bar trend of '80s and '90s Korea, when the thing to do was to hit the bar just one time, so you stacked everything you wanted on a small plate Jenga-style and hoped you and your two-foot-tall salad didn't crater on your way back to the table.

And it brings back my days on the other side of the counter when I was a banquet chef setting up salad bars for the buffet crowd.

The sense of adventure, danger, and ordered chaos are all here in this Big Fucking Salad, where you're going to build a big fucking salad with a variety of greens, vegetables sliced thin so they're easy to eat, fruit for different levels of sweetness, and different textures layered throughout to keep things interesting. This is a salad that's as fun to eat as it is to build.

SERVES 4 TO 6

½ head iceberg lettuce, chopped

1 cup loosely packed arugula

1 cup loosely packed baby spinach

1 cup diced cucumber

1 cup shaved broccoli

1 cup sliced red onions

1 cup sliced button mushrooms

1 cup grapes, halved (any color)

1 avocado, diced

1 apple, sliced (I like Fujis, but use any variety you like)

1 small orange or tangerine, zested and separated into segments

½ cup corn kernels, preferably fresh but you can do canned or frozen if that's what you got

Dijon Balsamic Vinaigrette (page 102)

½ cup shredded sharp cheddar cheese

1 cup toasted nuts, toasted bread crumbs, unsweetened granola, crushed saltines, or anything else to add crunch

A big handful of chopped mixed fresh herbs, such as basil, mint, cilantro, parsley, and dill

Salt and freshly ground black pepper

1. Bring out the biggest bowl you have. Add the lettuce, arugula, and spinach to form the base of the salad, then add the cucumber, broccoli, onions, mushrooms, grapes, avocado, apple slices, orange segments, and corn. Add a few big spoonfuls of dressing and toss. Add more dressing if needed.

2. Finish by sprinkling the orange zest all over, then the cheddar, whatever you're using for crunch, chopped herbs, a good pinch of salt and cracks of pepper, and enjoy your big fucking salad.

TUNA SALAD NIÇOISE
BIBIMBAP

I **always love Niçoise salads** . . . or, at least, I always love the ingredients on their own: the tuna, tomatoes, cucumber, olives, roasted potatoes, hard-boiled eggs, onions, green beans. But somehow, put them all together and, for me, the sum is never greater than its parts. And to someone who doesn't love eating salads, all these ingredients piled on a bed of Bibb lettuce might even look a little intimidating. To flip that, I want to hook you right into the salad, put you in the middle of the action. That action is the potato chips stepping in for the roasted potatoes. Then maybe you'll zoom out a little bit to see the pretty rainbow of colors of the vegetables and how everything is sitting on a cozy bed of rice that you can mix up as you would a bibimbap so you can eat it with a spoon. It's a salad, it's a rice bowl, whatever it is, it's unexpected in the very best way.

SERVES 4

4 large eggs

12 ounces green beans, trimmed

4 cups cooked rice, at room temperature

4 cups mixed greens (arugula, spinach, etc.)

2 (6.7-ounce) jars or 3 (5-ounce) cans tuna, preferably packed in oil, drained (see Get In Where You Fit In)

2 cups sliced red onions or shallots

2 cups cherry tomatoes, halved

2 cups diced radishes

1 cup minced green olives

2 cups diced cucumber

2 cups diced celery

2 avocados, diced

¼ cup chopped or torn fresh parsley

Dijon Balsamic Vinaigrette (page 102) or Old School Green Goddess (page 105)

Handful of potato chips, sea salt or salt and pepper flavor, crushed

1. Fill a large bowl with some ice and water and set aside. You'll need this for the boiled eggs and the blanched green beans.

2. Fill a medium pot with enough water to cover the eggs by an inch or two (but don't add the eggs just yet). Set the pot over medium-high heat. When it begins to gently boil, carefully add the eggs. Cook for 6 minutes, then use a slotted spoon to scoop out the eggs into the bowl of iced water so they stop cooking. Peel and put aside for now.

3. Return the pot of water to a boil. When it comes to a boil, drop in the green beans and boil for 2 to 3 minutes. The beans should be bright green and have some tenderness, but still be crisp. Transfer the beans to the ice bath. Once chilled, chop and set aside.

4. Now, start assembling. Set out four rice bowls. Divide the rice, mixed greens, tuna, red onions, tomatoes, radishes, olives, cucumber, celery, and avocados among the bowls. Halve the eggs and place one halved egg in each bowl along with some parsley. Generously spoon the dressing over everything and add the potato chips. Mix and eat like a rice bowl.

CHOICE WORDS: Potato chips on a field of green is designed to grab your attention, but on a deeper level, that's *The Choi of Cooking*. I get how hard it is for a lot of us to incorporate vegetables into our daily lives when it's not something we're used to doing. Meeting you where you are is a big part of my philosophy, and sometimes that means potato chips on a salad. No judgment.

Get In Where You Fit In

Who says a Niçoise has to have tuna? You can swap out the tuna for pretty much any other protein like tofu, grilled or rotisserie chicken, or a crispy salmon fillet (page 192).

If you like warm greens, or need a break from your salad routine, this is the salad to make. Romaine is, surprisingly, really great on the grill; it can take a little bit of char without falling apart, and its insides will become soft and cozy. Before serving, I throw a ton of herbs on top to brighten it up with some freshness. If you don't have a grill, or it's no longer grilling season, you also can char the romaine on a grill pan or nonstick skillet on the stovetop, or run it real quick under the broiler.

SERVES 4

2 heads romaine lettuce

Extra-virgin olive oil

Salt and freshly ground black pepper

½ cucumber, sliced or diced

Creamy Blue Cheese Dressing (page 107)

½ cup chopped roasted hazelnuts

½ cup chopped fresh basil

½ cup chopped fresh cilantro

1 tablespoon toasted sesame seeds, crushed

1. Preheat a grill to medium heat.

2. Slice each head of lettuce in half lengthwise through the stem. Coat each half in olive oil and season with salt and pepper.

3. Once the grill is hot, oil the grates and add the romaine cut-side down. Grill until the romaine is charred and tender, but not completely softened—you still want some crunch, just a few minutes. Flip the halves with tongs to warm the other side, about 1 minute.

4. To serve, plate a romaine half cut-side up on each of four plates or put them all on a large platter. Add the cucumbers and spoon the dressing all over. Garnish with the hazelnuts, basil, cilantro, sesame seeds, and another swirl of olive oil if you want, and serve.

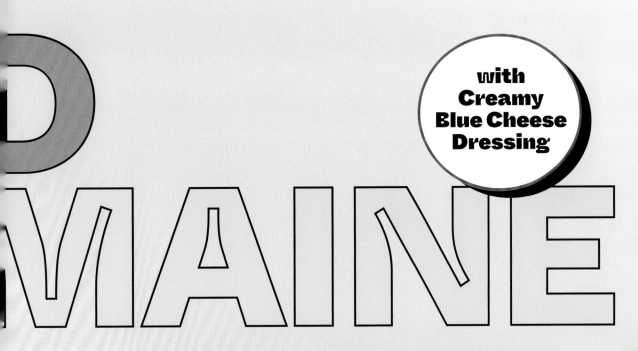

with Creamy Blue Cheese Dressing

D MAINE

EGGPLANT LAAB

I **think laab** (sometimes transliterated as larb) is one of the best and most approachable ways to eat a salad, because you're taking it in little by little, lettuce cup by lettuce cup. And the flavors are so bright and refreshing that you're constantly just going back for more, and before you know it, you've eaten a whole head of lettuce. It's often made with minced pork or another ground meat, but you'll find lots of nonmeat versions in Thai and Laotian kitchens, too. My version, inspired by all the great laab I've had over the years, goes the vegetable route and uses Thai eggplants as the base, with toasted sesame oil and a ton of different aromatics like lemongrass added in. And while the eggplant is cooked, it needs to be cooled and refrigerated before serving. So if you're planning ahead, be sure to build in a little time for the salad to chill out. You can make the laab a day before serving.

SERVES 4 TO 6

1 tablespoon toasted sesame oil

1¼ pounds Thai eggplant, minced or finely diced

Salt and freshly ground black pepper

2 tablespoons minced scallions

1 tablespoon minced lemongrass (see Lemongrass, page 34)

1 tablespoon minced garlic

1 tablespoon minced shallots

1 tablespoon minced fresh galangal or ginger

1 tablespoon minced Thai bird's eye chiles

2 tablespoons fish sauce

1 tablespoon soy sauce

1 tablespoon chili garlic sauce or sambal oelek

1 tablespoon toasted rice powder

1 tablespoon torn culantro (see Get In Where You Fit In)

2 tablespoons fresh cilantro, stems minced and leaves chopped

2 tablespoons fresh lime juice

Pinch of sugar

For serving (any or all): Puffed rice crackers, rice cakes, lettuce cups, cabbage wedges, sliced cucumbers, carrots halved or quartered

1. In a large skillet, warm the sesame oil over medium heat for 1 to 2 minutes. Add the eggplant and sauté until it starts to get some color and break down and soften (but not yet mushy), 4 to 5 minutes. Season with salt and pepper and stir.

2. Add the aromatics: the scallions, lemongrass, garlic, shallots, galangal, and chiles. Sauté for 2 to 3 more minutes. Add the fish sauce, soy sauce, chili garlic sauce, rice powder, and culantro.

3. Remove from the heat, give the eggplant a good stir, then add the cilantro stems and leaves, lime juice, and sugar. Let the eggplant cool in the pan for 5 minutes, then transfer to a large shallow plate and refrigerate for 15 to 20 minutes.

4. Serve the chilled laab with rice crackers or raw vegetables.

Get In Where You Fit In

- Culantro is a really intense cilantro-like herb that mellows out when cooked. Mexican and Asian markets may also call it spiny cilantro, Mexican coriander, sawtooth herb, or ngò gai. If you can't source it, use cilantro, mint, arugula, or basil instead.

- You can substitute Japanese eggplant for Thai eggplant. You also can use minced pork instead of the eggplant. If you use minced pork, it'll take a few minutes longer than the eggplant to brown and cook.

CACIO E PEPE
CAESAR SALAD

What if a salad actually tasted like a pasta dish? Answering that far-out stoner's question is how this salad came to be. This is basically a Caesar salad with the flavors of a cacio e pepe (the pasta with pepper and cheese) distilled into the dressing. It's savory and peppery, especially right at the end, and hits that pasta note without the pasta. Leftover dressing can be stored in a covered container for up to a week.

SERVES 4 TO 6

2 large egg yolks

1 cup mayonnaise

½ cup plus 1 tablespoon extra-virgin olive oil

¼ cup fresh lemon juice

1½ tablespoons chopped garlic

1 tablespoon chopped anchovies

1 tablespoon Worcestershire sauce

1 tablespoon minced yellow onion

2½ teaspoons freshly ground black pepper, plus more to taste

½ teaspoon mustard powder

½ tablespoon unsalted butter, at room temperature

½ cup grated Pecorino Romano or Parmesan cheese, plus a handful of shavings to finish

3 romaine hearts, leaves separated

Handful of croutons

1 lemon, cut into wedges

1. In a large bowl, whisk together the egg yolks, mayonnaise, ½ cup of the olive oil, the lemon juice, garlic, anchovies, Worcestershire sauce, onion, black pepper, and mustard powder.

2. Separately, in a small bowl, whisk together the remaining 1 tablespoon olive oil and 1 tablespoon water, then whisk in the butter (see Note). Add it to the rest of the dressing along with the cheese and whisk together. Taste. If it's a little too salty, add another splash or two of water. And add more pepper if you want.

3. Place the romaine leaves in a large bowl. Add the croutons and big spoonfuls of the dressing and toss with tongs or your hands to coat. Add more dressing if needed, then finish with a squeeze of lemon and a shower of shaved cheese. Serve with more lemon wedges so everyone can add more acid if they want.

NOTE: This is a small step, but don't skip it: Combining the oil and water, then whisking it with the butter, will help the dressing emulsify. If you happen to be making pasta to enjoy with the salad, you can use pasta water instead: Just whisk together 2 tablespoons of the pasta water with the butter, then add that to the dressing.

Get Dressed

Most salads for me have to be paired with a good dressing—otherwise, I'm going to get bored, I'm going to go and scrounge up something else to eat, I'm probably not coming back. So, to keep me in my seat, I have a few simple, delicious vinaigrettes and smooth, creamy dressings to outfit my greens. These are all dependable, reliable, and easy to make with what you probably already have in your kitchen. And as you make these over and over, I'll bet you'll start riffing on them to make them your own. And pretty soon, you'll want to make your own dressing to keep in your back pocket. For ideas on how to make your own vinaigrette, see page 108.

Dijon Balsamic Vinaigrette

MAKES ABOUT 2 CUPS

This balsamic dressing is designed to be an everything-everywhere dressing. It goes with delicate baby greens as easily as it does with sturdier romaine hearts. To make the dressing, it's easiest to throw all the ingredients into a blender, but you also can add everything to a large mason jar and give it a really good shake to emulsify.

1 cup extra-virgin olive oil

½ cup red wine vinegar

¼ cup balsamic vinegar

½ cup chopped fresh cilantro or parsley

1½ teaspoons Dijon mustard

1½ teaspoons minced garlic

Salt and freshly ground black pepper

In a blender, combine the olive oil, red wine vinegar, balsamic vinegar, cilantro, mustard, garlic, and good pinches of salt and pepper. Blend to combine and emulsify, 10 to 15 seconds. Taste and adjust the seasoning, then it's ready to dress.

Broken Orange Vinaigrette

MAKES 1 CUP

This is a "broken" vinaigrette in that it's not fully emulsified. In other words, you'll mix together the oils and acids, but they're not going to be completely combined. And that's on purpose: We want different tie-dyed spots of fat and flavor and citrus to pop through like a Whac-A-Mole. In addition to pouring this over roasted carrots, this also is a great, bright vinaigrette to toss with lettuce, spinach leaves, or arugula. Basically, this vinaigrette will turn any bowl of leafy greens into a quick salad.

½ cup extra-virgin olive oil

1 tablespoon grated orange zest

¼ cup freshly squeezed orange juice (about 1 medium orange)

1 tablespoon grated lemon zest

2 tablespoons fresh lemon juice

1 tablespoon red wine vinegar

1 tablespoon minced garlic

1 tablespoon minced fresh ginger and its juice

1 teaspoon Dijon mustard

1 heaping teaspoon honey

Freshly ground black pepper

A handful of chopped fresh herbs, such as thyme, basil, and mint

In a medium bowl, whisk together the olive oil, orange zest, orange juice, lemon zest, lemon juice, vinegar, garlic, ginger (and juice), mustard, honey, and lots of cracked black pepper just to combine. Add the herbs and stir. Use immediately, or place in an airtight container and refrigerate for up to 3 days.

The Orange Bang Vinaigrette

MAKES ABOUT 3 CUPS

There was a whole period in my life where I thought Orange Bang and Orange Julius were healthy because they had orange juice in them. I'd spend the day looking forward to having one of those drinks because I thought it'd improve my life—and it was damn tasty! Of course, I grew up and realized it was all processed sugars and not nearly as healthy as I thought it was. Still, I love the flavor. This vinaigrette is designed after those orange drinks, except instead of drinking it, we're going to put it on a salad. *This* will improve your life.

5 whole garlic cloves, peeled

⅔ cup orange juice, home-squeezed (2 to 3 oranges) or store-bought

½ cup rice vinegar

¼ cup soy sauce

1½ tablespoons yellow miso paste

1½ tablespoons sugar

2½ teaspoons minced fresh ginger

2½ teaspoons chili oil

Juice of ½ lime

Salt and freshly ground black pepper

1¼ cups vegetable oil

In a blender, combine the garlic, orange juice, vinegar, soy sauce, miso, sugar, ginger, chili oil, lime juice, and a pinch of salt and pepper. Blend for about 10 seconds, then, while blending, drizzle in the vegetable oil. Dress your salad, or pour it into a jar or other container with a lid and keep it in the fridge for up to 1 week.

Get In Where You Fit In

Try adding a jalapeño for some heat, some cilantro or a little more lime for some brightness and acidity, or some shredded carrots for sweetness.

Old School Green Goddess

MAKES 3 CUPS

Green Goddess dressing feels like a throwback to the *Brady Bunch* era, but every time you have it on a salad, it's herby, it's fresh—you can't ever be mad at it. This is a creamy dressing that just never goes out of style; it holds its own and has its place in every generation. My version really leans into the herby part of the dressing: I use scallions, parsley, basil, spinach, cilantro, mint, chives, even some tarragon and dill for a constellation of bright flavors, with yogurt and mayonnaise for body. One hundred, two hundred years from now, I bet Green Goddess dressings will still be around, and maybe this one will stand the test of time, too.

½ cup plain yogurt (any type)

½ cup mayonnaise

½ cup sliced or chopped scallions

½ cup fresh parsley (sprigs and leaves, all of it)

½ cup loosely packed fresh basil

½ cup loosely packed baby spinach

½ cup fresh cilantro (sprigs and leaves, all of it)

¼ cup fresh mint leaves

¼ cup fresh chives

3 tablespoons champagne vinegar

2 tablespoons minced garlic

½ tablespoon capers

Grated zest of 1 lemon

Juice of 1 or 2 lemons

Fresh tarragon

Fresh dill

Salt and freshly ground black pepper

½ cup extra-virgin olive oil

In a blender, combine the yogurt, mayonnaise, scallions, parsley, basil, spinach, cilantro, mint, chives, vinegar, garlic, capers, lemon zest, juice of 1 lemon, and heavy pinches of tarragon, dill, salt, and pepper. Blend for 10 to 15 seconds, then slowly add the olive oil. Puree until combined; the texture will be a little loose, and that's okay. Taste and add more lemon juice if you want, and adjust the seasoning if needed. It's best fresh, but you can store leftovers for a few days in a jar or lidded container in your fridge.

Bonus Round

You can turn this dressing into a dip for things like crudités and crackers by thickening it up with a little more mayo or adding some sour cream to give it some body.

Lemon Ranch Dressing

MAKES 3 CUPS

We've grown up ruled by bottled ranch dressings. But ranch can be made from scratch with fresh herbs and stuff you probably have in your pantry, and it'll be better than what you can get at the store. I make this dressing for Grilled Artichoke and Zucchini (page 70), but it's also great as a dip for raw vegetables on a crudités platter or tossed with a bowl of greens. It will make any vegetable instantly delicious, and for that reason I think it's worth the few minutes it takes to make this ranch from scratch. Once made, the dressing will keep, covered and refrigerated, for 1 week.

1½ cups sour cream

1 cup mayonnaise

Grated zest and juice of ½ large or 1 small lemon

¼ cup extra-virgin olive oil

1 tablespoon champagne vinegar

1 tablespoon minced fresh dill, plus more for garnish

1½ teaspoons minced fresh chives, plus more for garnish

1½ teaspoons minced scallions

1½ teaspoons chopped fresh parsley, plus more for garnish

1 teaspoon minced garlic

1 tablespoon toasted sesame seeds

½ teaspoon garlic powder

Salt and freshly ground black pepper

MSG (optional)

In a large bowl, combine the sour cream, mayonnaise, lemon zest, lemon juice, oil, vinegar, dill, chives, scallions, parsley, minced garlic, sesame seeds, garlic powder, and pinches of salt and pepper. Stir to combine. Taste and adjust seasoning. You can even throw a small pinch of MSG in there if you'd like. To serve, place in a bowl and garnish with herbs.

Creamy Blue Cheese Dressing

MAKES ABOUT 2 CUPS

Creamy dressings are always good dressings to have around, because they're delicious crowd-pleasers—you can't really go wrong with them. Blue cheese dressing is especially good to have on hand, because it is so versatile: It can stand up to any ingredient in a salad; it doubles as a dip for vegetables, chicken wings (page 206), or chicken nuggets (page 208), and it triples as a sandwich spread. Even if the pungency of blue cheese usually turns you off, try it here in a different form as a dressing combined with a bunch of familiar ingredients. You might like it after all.

1 to 2 cups finely crumbled blue cheese, to taste

¼ cup mayonnaise

¼ cup sour cream

¼ cup buttermilk

¼ cup chopped fresh parsley

½ cup minced scallions

¼ cup minced fresh chives

1 tablespoon fresh lemon juice

1 tablespoon red wine vinegar

½ tablespoon Tabasco sauce

½ tablespoon Worcestershire sauce

½ tablespoon minced garlic

1 tablespoon extra-virgin olive oil

Salt and freshly ground black pepper

In a large bowl, gently whisk together 1 cup of the blue cheese, the mayonnaise, sour cream, buttermilk, parsley, scallions, chives, lemon juice, vinegar, Tabasco, Worcestershire sauce, and garlic. Taste and add up to another 1 cup of blue cheese if you want. Once combined, whisk in the olive oil and salt and pepper to taste. Set aside, or refrigerate until ready to use. It can be stored in the fridge in a jar or other airtight container for 1 week.

ETTE in 7 STEPS or Less

There are a million bottles of salad dressings at the market, so it can seem like dressings are the most complicated or time-consuming thing to make. But they are actually one of the easiest and fastest things to make, and it's very easy to make them very delicious. Take the vinaigrette we made at Kogi, for example. That had to be simple, or else there was just no way we could have made it on the truck. Pretty much the most complicated thing about it was finding an outlet in the wild in the middle of the night, so we could plug in our blender and make a new batch on the fly between stops. And that vinaigrette was fucking amazing.

At the end of the day, and at its most basic, a vinaigrette is just an oil and a vinegar that you combine, season with salt and pepper, and eat with a bowl of greens, or mix with the slaw on a taco, or pour over vegetables, or use as a dip with crusty bread, or all of the above. You could add more ingredients to it if you want, but you don't have to, and you can easily adjust it based on where you are and what you have around.

On a bigger level, you learn a lot by making a vinaigrette. You learn how to taste, you learn how to season, you learn how to balance, you learn the role of acids in a dish. Basically, you learn how to get in the kitchen and build. You learn how to cook.

To make your own vinaigrette, you can, but don't need to, memorize a specific recipe. It's much more about the method and the technique than it is about specific measurements. And I mean that: You don't even need measuring spoons. You can use a soup spoon or a little plastic salsa cup—basically, anything is fine as long it's clean and gives you some way to measure consistently. Then, after making a few vinaigrettes, you won't even need that. You'll be able to bring it all together on taste and feel alone.

Vinaigrette Basics

 Choose an oil

Anything that tastes good. If you're really stuck, you can't go wrong with extra-virgin olive oil to start. Other good options:

Flavorful oils
- Avocado oil
- Coconut oil
- Walnut oil
- Toasted sesame oil
- Chili oil
- Truffle oil

More neutral-tasting oils
- Grapeseed oil
- Corn oil
- Safflower oil
- Sunflower oil

If you choose something that tastes pretty strong, like toasted sesame oil or chili oil, a little will go a long way, so pair it up with a more neutral oil and taste the two together until it's as nice as you'd like.

 Choose an acid

Usually, this will be some type of vinegar or citrus. Some vinegars are pretty mellow, some are pretty sharp. Same with citrus: Different varieties of orange, for example, have different levels of acidity. Some lemons are real puckers and some aren't. Keep tasting. A few examples of each:

Vinegars
- Apple cider vinegar
- Sherry vinegar
- Champagne vinegar
- Rice vinegar
- Red wine vinegar
- Balsamic vinegar

Citrus
- Lemon juice
- Orange juice
- Lime juice
- Yuzu juice

 Get the salt and black pepper

Kosher salt at the very least. If you really get into it, Himalayan pink salt and sea salt bring a different type of saltiness to the dressing.

And, of course, ground black pepper, preferably freshly ground.

 Combine, season, taste

Generally, I like to start with twice as much oil as acid. So, if you're using a soup spoon, measure two or three spoonfuls of oil into a bowl or jar and add one spoonful of acid. If it's too acidic for your liking, add a little more oil.

Add a good pinch of salt and pepper and whisk it all together. Taste and adjust the seasoning. This vinaigrette is good as is, so once you get the proportion of everything right, you can scale it up to make as much as you need and skip to step 6. Or you can continue to the next step and add a few more layers of flavor.

Pick your add-ons

From here, you can have a lot of fun adding different flavor components to your vinaigrette. For each of these, you want to add to taste, so add a bit at a time and keep tasting.

For sweetness (or to take the acidity down a notch)
- Agave syrup
- Brown sugar
- Cane sugar
- Honey
- Maple syrup

For umami
- Fish sauce
- Liquid aminos
- Miso paste
- Parmesan cheese
- Ponzu sauce
- Soy sauce

For heat
- Gochugaru
- Hot sauce
- Jalapeño slices
- Red pepper flakes

For creaminess and to help emulsify the dressing:
- Mustard, any type
- Avocado
- Carrots, grated

- Crème fraîche
- Daikon, grated
- Mayonnaise
- Nut butters, such as peanut or almond
- Nutritional yeast
- Pesto (page 245)
- Sour cream
- Tahini
- Yogurt, thick

Other ideas
- Fresh herbs, like basil, parsley, cilantro, tarragon, rosemary, mint, dill, and oregano
- Garlic, minced or roasted
- Ginger, grated
- Onions, red or yellow, minced or thinly sliced
- Scallions, minced or thinly sliced
- Shallots, minced
- Spices like ground fennel, paprika, or smoked paprika

 Separate or together?

When I was coming up as a chef, I was taught that the "proper" way to make a vinaigrette is to drizzle the oil into the vinegar slowly, drop by drop, whisking the whole way until the two completely combined and became silky smooth. That's one way to do it, but that isn't the only way or the easiest way to emulsify a vinaigrette. Some people like to put everything into a jar, screw on the lid, and shake it up. Me, I like to add everything to a blender, especially if I'm using a bunch of different ingredients. Blend until the vinaigrette is luxurious and shiny and a bunch of what I call "friendship bubbles" dot the surface that show the oil and vinegar have made it to another level.

You also can make a "broken" vinaigrette, where you whisk everything together but don't get total emulsification. It's a taste thing: Sometimes, especially for salads, you want your vinaigrette to be completely smooth and uniform so every part of the greens gets every part of the dressing. Sometimes, like in Broken Orange Vinaigrette (page 103), the separate, uneven bursts of oil and fat from a less fully combined dressing is what you want throughout the dish. It really just depends on what you're making and what you're going for.

Put It All Together

 Make your own vinaigrette

Take the oil, vinegar, salt, pepper, the additional flavors you're using and whisk it, shake it, blend it, whatever works for you. Taste the vinaigrette with whatever you're pairing it with; for a salad, for example, take a leaf of something and dip it in the vinaigrette. Taste and adjust and repeat until it's where you want.

And you've made a vinaigrette. And it's your very own. And you'll be able to make it next time.

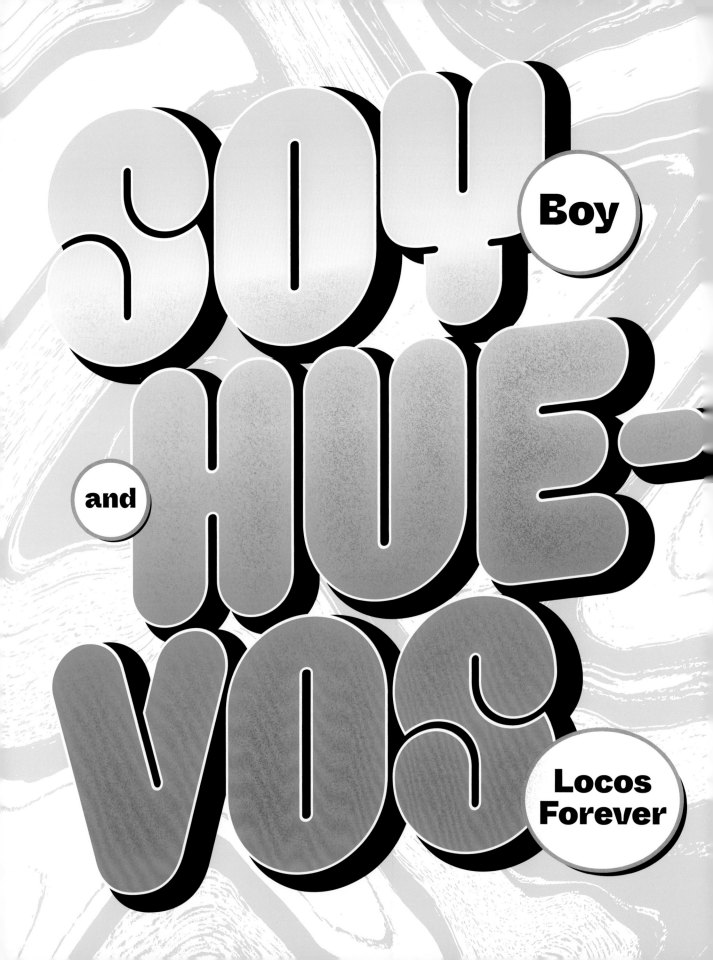

Tofu and eggs are the real MVPs in the kitchen. They do everything: They can go from a little snack to the main part of a meal. They can be one dish among many on a table, or be that extra thing you need to finish a dish. But because tofu and eggs are always around, I think sometimes we end up taking them for granted and don't give them the credit they're due. So, in this chapter, we're going to give these two humble ingredients the spotlight to celebrate their versatility and create whole worlds with them.

What makes both tofu and eggs such clutch players is that they are simple, satisfying protein options that don't need a lot of preparation and can only be made more delicious, even totally transformed, with a bit of technique and some helper sauces. Some of these, like Tofu Breakfast Burritos (page 118) and Deviled Egg Sandos (page 128), are simple meals all on their own. Others, like Drunken Kimchi Tofu Sifu (page 116) and Egg Drop Top Soup (page 130), are quick snacks on their own, or, with the addition of a bowl of rice, some kimchi or pickles, or a salad or vegetable dish, can be part of a full spread.

If you don't know what to make on any given day, tofu or eggs or both will probably be your answer. Keep them in your fridge for always.

COLD
AND C

Cold tofu with soy sauce is a staple. For me, it's what I imagine cottage cheese and peaches, or yogurt and fruit, is for some other people, something that you can make real quick on the go as a snack, but in a savory rather than sweet sort of way. It also can be an appetizer or part of a spread of banchan and other side dishes to round out a meal of steamed pork belly (page 218) or grilled meats or vegetables. Plus it's a great blank slate for other toppings. Try it, say, with some chopped kimchi right on top.

SERVES 4

1 (14-ounce) package soft or silken tofu

½ cup Soy-Ginger Sauce (page 244) or Korean Crying Tiger Sauce (page 246)

Minced fresh chives, for garnish

Freshly ground black pepper

Toasted sesame seeds, for garnish

Flaky sea salt

Drain the tofu, then pat it dry with a paper towel. Slice it crosswise into 1-inch-thick steaks. Shingle them on a plate. Gently ladle the sauce over the tofu, then shower with a shit-ton of minced chives. Add a few cracks of black pepper, the sesame seeds, and a pinch of flaky salt on top, and serve.

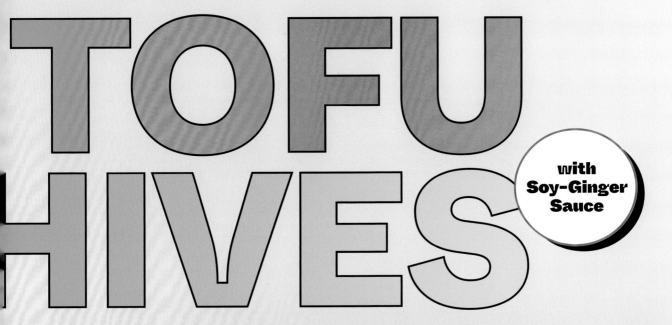

TOFU HIVES

with Soy-Ginger Sauce

DRUNKEN KIMCHI TOFU SIFU

When someone's a sifu, they're the number one, the master, the mentor, the one you respect above all. I call this dish—crisped tofu topped with buttery kimchi—sifu because this recipe teaches you some fundamentals of cooking: how to sear, how to caramelize, how to concentrate flavor, all in a few simple motions. You can study this as a form and always learn something. It's unbreakable in that way. Oh, and it's drunken not because there's alcohol in it, but because it's part of a whole category of Korean dishes called anju, which refers to foods you pick at in between shots of soju. But you don't have to drink soju or any other alcohol to eat this. I ate this in huge bites as a kid. No alcohol. Just food drunk. You can be food drunk with this with huge bites and be done with it, or eat it with some rice, or some rice plus a bowl of soup.

SERVES 4

1 (14-ounce) package firm tofu

½ cup all-purpose flour

Salt and freshly ground black pepper

2 large eggs

Toasted sesame oil

Butter Kimchi Jam (page 254), warmed, or store-bought kimchi

Minced scallions, for garnish

1. Drain the tofu, then slice it crosswise into ½-inch-thick steaks. Completely dry each slice with a paper towel. I mean completely; to get a good crisp on the tofu, it's got to be as dry as you can get it.

2. Season the flour with salt and pepper and place on a shallow plate or baking sheet. Crack the eggs into a shallow bowl and beat.

3. In a medium skillet, warm 2 teaspoons sesame oil over medium heat.

4. Add a few slices of tofu to the seasoned flour and dredge them lightly. When the sesame oil in the pan begins to shimmer, dredge the tofu in the eggs and place them in the pan. Add only as many as you can without overcrowding the pan, so the tofu will sear nicely.

5. Cook until the tofu steaks are lightly browned and crispy on each side, 3 to 5 minutes per side. Move the tofu to a plate. Repeat with the remaining tofu, adding more sesame oil as necessary.

6. To serve, spoon the butter kimchi jam over the top of the tofu and garnish with minced scallions.

TOFU BREAKFAST BURRITOS

The tofu burrito was one of the early mainstays on Kogi's menu, and part of the reason why it's stuck around for so long is because it satisfies whether you eat meat or not. Tofu and scrambled eggs share a similar texture, so if you're not really into tofu, or you think meat has to be part of every meal, you can almost sneak the tofu into the burrito without even realizing it. And before you know it, you have a really great vegetarian breakfast burrito, and you're eating a little less meat without sacrificing the flavor or the experience.

MAKES 2 BURRITOS (10-INCH TORTILLAS) OR 4 BURRITOS (8-INCH TORTILLAS)

Extra-virgin olive oil

One-third of a 14-ounce package soft, medium, or firm tofu (about 4½ ounces), drained and diced

1 tablespoon unsalted butter

Salt and freshly ground black pepper

½ to ¾ cup leftover Crispy Mashed Potatoes (page 82), or store-bought frozen hash browns or Tater Tots cooked according to the package directions

3 large eggs, beaten

2 (10-inch) or 4 (8-inch) flour tortillas

Shredded cheddar cheese

Tons of chopped fresh cilantro

Salsa Verde (page 250) and/or Salsa Roja (page 251)

Tapatío or your favorite hot sauce

1. In a large nonstick skillet or sauté pan, heat 3 tablespoons of oil over medium heat. When it begins to get glossy and shimmer, add the tofu. Get a little sizzle on the tofu, about 30 seconds, then add the butter and season with salt and pepper. The butter will begin to brown and smell a little nutty. Add as much of the potatoes as you want, breaking them up into smaller pieces as they go in.

2. Reduce the heat to medium-low, pour the eggs in and scramble, stirring the eggs and shaking the pan to emulsify and keep the eggs airy and light. Cook until the eggs are just set and soft, 15 to 20 seconds, then take the pan off the heat.

3. In another large pan, add a kiss of olive oil. Place a tortilla, bumpier-side down, into the pan and cook until it's blistered but still pliable, then flip. Add a handful of cheddar along the lower third of the tortilla, then some of the tofu scramble, more cheese on top if you want, and finally some cilantro, a few spoonfuls of the salsa, and a dash or two of Tapatío. Carefully slide it off the pan and onto a cutting board or large plate, tuck in the sides and roll roll roll.

4. Repeat to make the remaining burritos.

Power Up

Pull back on the carbs by omitting the potatoes. You can go one step further and eliminate the tortilla, too, and turn this into a breakfast bowl instead of a breakfast burrito.

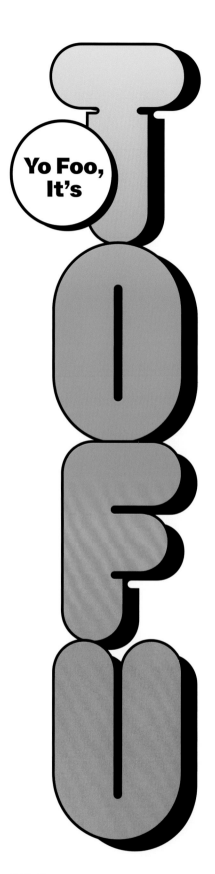

Yo Foo, It's TOFU

I look back on all my years growing up with tofu as the rings in my tree trunk. It was just like bread to me. What I mean is that tofu was always there, and it could be eaten in so many different ways: cold, toasted, pan-fried, crumbled, in salads, in soup, in a lettuce wrap, as croutons, as a sandwich "meat," baked. It was an anytime food; you could have it before school, for school, after school. Breakfast, brunch, lunch, linner, dinner, midnight munchies.

I have a bunch of tofu dishes in this chapter and elsewhere in the book, but tofu has so many lives that once you get the hang of using it, you'll use it everywhere. You just need to know how to work with it.

TYPES OF TOFU

Tofu's basically soy milk with a coagulant added to thicken it up. The texture of tofu ranges from extra soft to pretty firm, depending on whether, and how much, water is pressed out of it. The more water is pressed out, the firmer the tofu.

I use a range of tofu types in my recipes, from soft and silken to medium and firm, and as you cook through the recipes, you'll see and taste the difference between all of them: The soft and silken tofus dance in their containers and are so soft and creamy that you can put a spoon through it and eat it just like that. Yum. Firm tofu, though, doesn't wiggle as much. It's more solid and good for searing and frying.

PREPPING TOFU

Most of the tofu you'll use for the book are packaged with water to keep it fresh. Drain the water before using the tofu.

USING TOFU

Which tofu you use depends on what you're going to use it for.

SOME WAYS TO USE SOFT TOFU:

- Slice it up and eat it up as a snack, like in the Cold Tofu and Chives with Soy-Ginger Sauce (page 114).
- Fill up a burrito (page 118) or a taco.
- Dice and add to soups or stews.
- Add it to scrambled eggs.

SOME WAYS TO USE MEDIUM AND FIRM TOFUS:

- Dice and add it to soups or stews, like in Bomb Kha Chowder (page 138), My Boo (page 142), and Braised Spicy Korean Chicken (page 210).
- Fill up a burrito (page 118) or a taco.
- Work it into the filling in Not Shrimp Toast but Think Shrimp Toast, Okay? OK! (page 226), or in dumplings or meatballs.
- Crumble the tofu over a salad.
- Sauté the tofu with vegetables or with Butter Kimchi Jam (page 254).
- Use it in Green Bean and Chicken Stir-Fry (page 202) instead of the chicken, or toss it in any other stir-fry or fried rice.
- Slice and sear the tofu and wrap it in lettuce, put it in a sandwich, or tuck it into an onigiri (page 168).
- Add it to your rice bowl.
- Dredge the tofu in flour and pan-fry it like in the Drunken Kimchi Tofu Sifu (page 116), or cut the tofu into sticks, then dredge to turn 'em into tofu fries.

IF YOU'RE GOING TO SEAR OR FRY THE TOFU,

take the time to do one more step and squeeze out the water by pressing the tofu between a bunch of paper towels. Or, if it works for what you're making, you can crumble the tofu, place the crumbles in a cheesecloth, and squeeze the water out that way. The goal is to get the tofu as dry as possible so it'll sear or fry up real nice—and not steam—once it hits the hot pan.

IF YOU DON'T USE ALL THE TOFU IN THE PACKAGE,

place it in an airtight container and cover with water. Use it the next day if possible, but if you can't, it'll keep for around 5 days as long as you drain and replace the water each day.

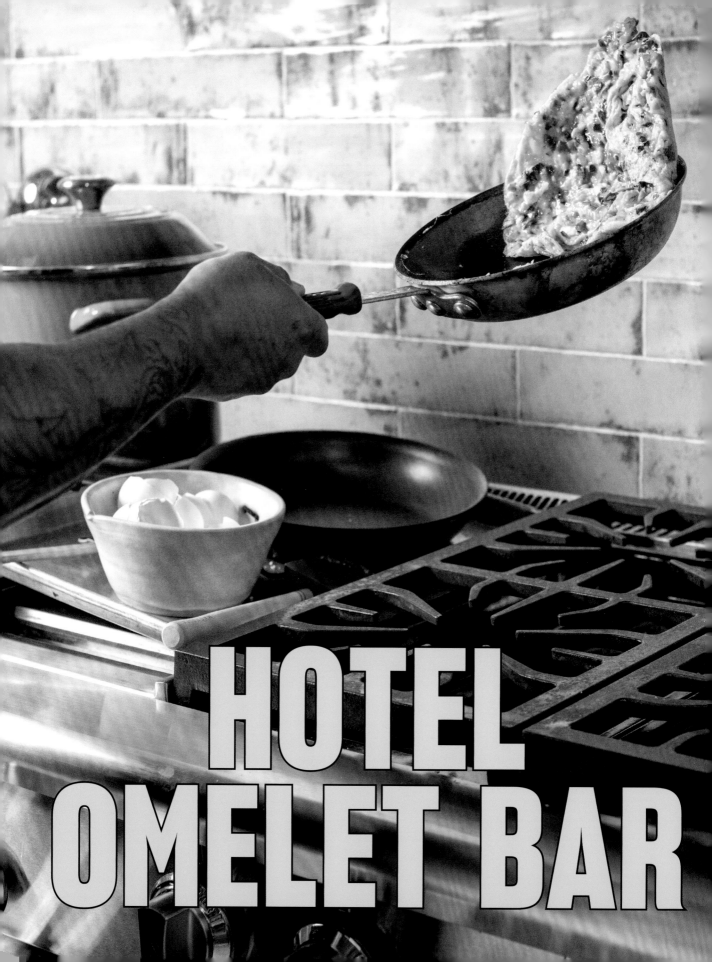

HOTEL
OMELET BAR

Back in the earlier part of my cooking career, I had a great run overseeing the food program for the Embassy Suites' West Coast hotels. One of the things we did was to develop a fucking great omelet bar, which might sound a little pedestrian or even boring, but there is a real art and craft to making a great omelet. In front of that little omelet pan, all your powers as a cook come into play: You need to be able to control the heat (so the eggs set just right), multitask (you're controlling the heat *while* you keep the eggs moving so they become puffy and airy), and be present with laser focus on your station (it's a thin line between an undercooked and an overcooked omelet). It's not easy, and there's no better practice than just making a bunch of omelets one right after another. This recipe puts you in charge of the omelet station for the day to make the same kind of American hotel-style omelets we made, where the omelet is folded, not rolled like some fancy French ones.

MAKES 6 OMELETS

½ pound bacon, minced

Extra-virgin olive oil

6 tablespoons minced scallions

6 tablespoons minced yellow onion

6 tablespoons minced red bell pepper

6 tablespoons minced mushrooms (any variety you like)

6 tablespoons minced plum tomatoes

Salt and freshly ground black pepper

1 cup baby spinach, chopped

18 large eggs (3 large eggs per omelet), beaten

Shredded cheddar cheese

Hot sauce, for serving

Get In Where You Fit In

You can use egg whites instead of whole eggs if you want.

1. In an 8-inch nonstick skillet, cook the bacon over high heat until crispy and delicious, a few minutes. Set aside on paper towels to drain.

2. Wipe out the pan and add a good swirl of oil. Add 1 tablespoon each of bacon, scallions, onion, bell pepper, mushrooms, and tomato.

3. Season everything with salt and pepper and sauté until you start to see some color and caramelization on the vegetables, about 1 minute. Add a handful of spinach and cook just until the spinach wilts, then drop the heat to medium-low.

4. Add 6 ounces (about ½ cup) of beaten eggs and swirl the eggs around the pan. Keep swirling. As the eggs set, tilt the pan and lift up the curds with a spatula so the uncooked eggs flow under the cooked parts and the eggs puff up. When the egg is lightly golden and the liquid is 80 percent dissipated, flip the omelet. Do the best you can; you'll get the hang of it with more practice. Immediately add a handful of cheddar in the center. And just as the cheese begins to melt, flip the omelet over itself like you're closing a book and slide it onto a plate. Serve it up with the hot sauce on the table.

5. Repeat. Repeat. Repeat. You're the omelet chef today.

OMELET FOR ONE: You master the omelet station real quick when you make one right after another, but if you're not feeding a big party, you can easily downsize this recipe. To make one omelet, the directions for cooking are the same but reduce the ingredients to 3 large eggs, whisked; 1 ounce (1 slice) bacon, minced; 1 tablespoon each minced scallions, yellow onion, red bell pepper, mushroom, and plum tomato; a handful of chopped baby spinach, salt and pepper, and shredded cheddar.

KOREAN STEAMED EGG
SOUFFLÉ

Every Korean kid grows up with this egg dish. It's embedded in our DNA. It unites East Coast and West Coast. It'll take us home no matter where we are. The idea behind it is simple: Scramble eggs, pour them in a ttukbaegi (a Korean earthenware pot) with some water and seasonings, cover, and poof, it'll puff up like a soufflé. My mom always put the eggs in, turned the heat to way high, and it was perfect by the time we were at the table. I can never do that without overcooking or burning the eggs, so I have to go low and slow. Even at low and slow though, it's a very thin line between uncooked and overcooked, so keep an eye on it. It'll feel like forever, but it'll be done in about 20 minutes. With a bowl of steamed rice, and maybe some kimchi and dried seaweed, this is a meal. You don't have to top it with the caviar, but it adds that little extra extra.

SERVES 2

4 large eggs

1 cup minced scallions

1 tablespoon toasted sesame oil

1 tablespoon soy sauce

Generous pinch of freshly ground black pepper

Ikura caviar (optional)

Flaky sea salt (optional)

1. Crack the eggs into a medium bowl and beat well. Whisk in ½ cup water, the scallions, sesame oil, soy sauce, and pepper. Pour the eggs into a small (2½-cup) ttukbaegi or a 20-ounce cocotte, Dutch oven, clay pot, or any pot that has a lid and that can be heated on the stove (see Get In Where You Fit In). Bring to a very light boil, then drop the heat to low and cover.

2. Take a quick peek under the lid after about 8 minutes to see if the egg has started to puff up and soufflé and set (the top may still be a little runny). If it has, remove the lid. If not, continue to cook for a few more minutes. Once the lid is removed, continue to cook, still nice and gentle on low, until the water has evaporated, 10 to 15 more minutes.

3. Increase the heat to high for 1 minute to finish cooking, then turn off the heat, re-cover, and let it sit for 2 to 3 minutes to set.

4. Remove the lid. If desired, add caviar right on top and a sprinkle of sea salt. Serve with a big spoon.

Get In Where You Fit In + Choice Words

If you don't have a pot that's similar to what I use, that's okay! You can use one that's a little smaller or even a little bigger than 20 ounces, in which case my cook times will differ from yours. This is a great dish to practice *cooking* as opposed to just following a recipe: Read through the recipe to pick up the method, then zoom in and focus on what's going on in the pot. Use your senses, not your watch, to tell you what your steamed egg needs. And yeah, despite your best intentions, you might overcook the egg. That's okay. Intentions count. It's still going to be good. And I bet it'll be even better the next time.

Shiitake Goat Cheese **FRIT**

My version of frittata is basically an open-faced omelet that starts as a soft scramble on the stove and finishes with a bit of puff and golden color from the oven. This is a chameleon of a dish: It can morph and match its surroundings. With some OJ and coffee, it's breakfast. Dressed up with a nice salad, it's a Sunday brunch. Omit the goat cheese and drape it over a mound of fried rice and it'll give omurice vibes. A cast-iron skillet or a pan with straight sides, like a sauté pan, will help the frittata keep its shape, but don't sweat it if you don't have one. It'll work with whatever ovenproof pan you have. This makes for a perfect solo meal, but if you want to serve two or three people, you can double the ingredients. Since it will be thicker than the one you would make for one, it'll take a few minutes longer to cook.

SERVES 1

Extra-virgin olive oil

1 cup sliced shiitake mushrooms

Salt and freshly ground black pepper

3 large eggs

¼ cup milk or heavy cream

1 sprig fresh thyme, leaves picked

1 heaping tablespoon minced fresh chives

1 teaspoon unsalted butter, cut into a few small pieces

¼ cup crumbled goat cheese

Hot sauce, for serving

1. Preheat the oven to 375°F.

2. In a medium cast-iron skillet or ovenproof nonstick sauté pan, heat 1 tablespoon of olive oil over medium heat. When it begins to shimmer, add the sliced mushrooms and cook until the mushrooms start to brown, 2 to 3 minutes. Season with salt and pepper and sauté until the mushrooms are browned all over, 2 to 3 minutes. Place the mushrooms in a bowl to cool.

3. When the mushrooms are cool, beat the eggs in a large bowl. Add the mushrooms, milk, thyme, chives, a big pinch of salt and pepper, and a splash of water.

4. Wipe your skillet clean and place back over medium heat. Add 2 to 3 tablespoons of olive oil, or enough to coat the bottom of the pan. Add the eggs, swirling them and tilting the pan as curds form to get a soft scramble. Just as all of the liquid starts to set, dot the surface of the eggs with the butter and goat cheese and pop the pan into the oven.

5. Bake until the frittata is lightly caramelized and browned and the cheese and butter are melty, 7 to 10 minutes.

6. Cool the frittata for a few minutes, slide the whole thing onto a large plate, and serve it up at the table with the hot sauce.

Power Up
Swap out the whole eggs for egg whites and the frittata still will be damn tasty.

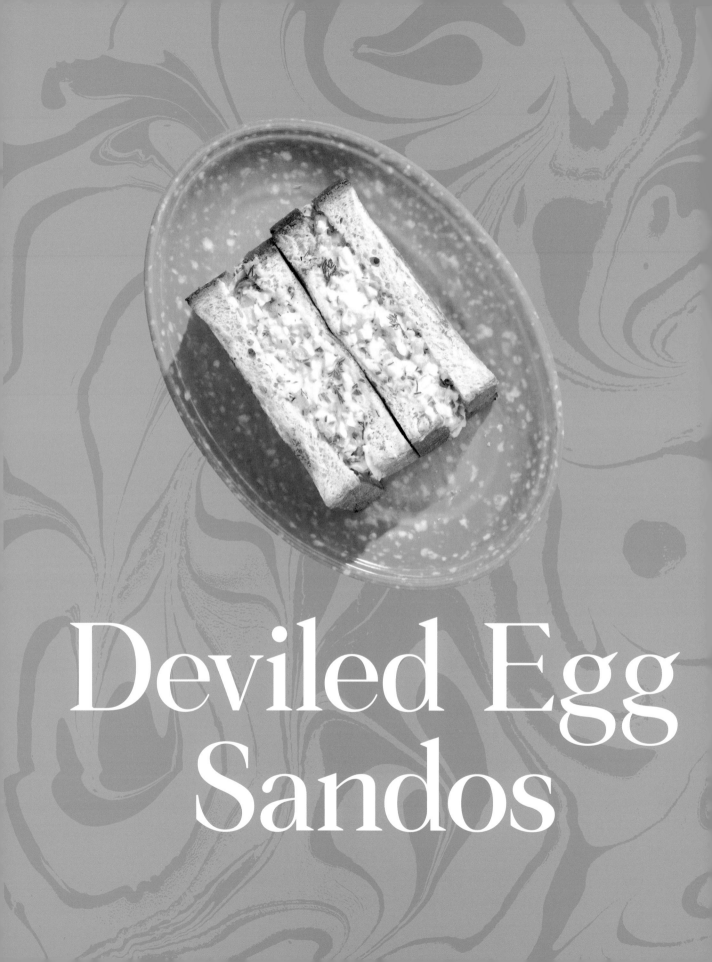

Deviled Egg
Sandos

Egg salad sandwiches were not part of my mom's repertoire, so it's not something I really was super familiar with as a kid. In fact, it wasn't until Jonathan Gold (RIP; pour one out for Mr. Gold) talked up the version at this spot around here called Europane that I finally understood what can happen when you combine hard-boiled eggs with mayonnaise: magic. The eggs become smooth and creamy, similar to the texture of a deviled egg, then the herbs and celery step in to lift everything with freshness and crunch. This egg salad sandwich is an homage to that egg salad sandwich, with some inspiration from the Japanese-style versions that use Kewpie mayo and slices of milk bread.

MAKES 4 SANDWICHES

6 large eggs

½ cup Kewpie mayonnaise

1½ teaspoons yellow or Dijon mustard

½ lemon

½ cup minced scallions

½ cup minced fresh chives

½ cup minced celery

1 tablespoon minced fresh dill

Extra-virgin olive oil

Champagne, rice, or apple cider vinegar

Salt and freshly ground black pepper

Tabasco or your favorite hot sauce

Unsalted butter, at room temperature

8 slices milk bread or white sandwich bread

1. Set up a large bowl with a bunch of ice and water. Bring a pot of water to a boil over high heat. Gently add the eggs and boil for 11 minutes. Pull the eggs out of the boiling water and transfer them directly into the ice bath.

2. When cool enough to handle, peel the eggs, halve them, and separate the yolks and the whites. Place the yolks in a blender or a small food processor with the mayonnaise and mustard. Puree until smooth.

3. In a large bowl, use a fork to chop the egg whites up into a bunch of pieces. Add the yolk puree, along with a small squeeze of the lemon, the scallions, chives, celery, dill, a drizzle of olive oil, a splash of vinegar, a pinch of salt and pepper, and a dash of hot sauce. Gently now, mix everything together. Taste, then add more lemon juice if you'd like, and adjust the seasoning.

4. Set a medium or large skillet over low heat. Lightly butter one side of each bread slice, then place them, buttered-side down, into the pan. Lightly toast the bread—just that buttered side, so don't flip the slices. You want just a bit of browning, or just enough for a little texture, but not so much that you lose their pillowy softness.

5. Remove the bread. Dividing evenly, spread the egg salad over the untoasted side of 4 slices of toast, then close the sandwich with the other slices. Slice into rectangles or triangles, whatever makes you happy, and enjoy.

EGG DROP SOUP TOP

Everyone makes their egg drop soup a little differently, so my version might be (probably is) different from what you like to get at your favorite Chinese restaurant. But hopefully, it evokes the same feeling, because, to me, egg drop soup is one of the most simply regal soups in the world. You're making a soup out of a quick chicken stock, and then you're transforming it by dropping an egg into the broth and basically souffléing it. Even with the bunch of vegetables I add, it still comes together so fast that you can easily make it part of any meal, or you can cook it up as a quick snack—a snack that's better than a lot of the candy bars, bags of chips, overly salted trail mixes, and other empty calories a lot of us grew up reaching for.

Power Up
Swap out the whole eggs for just the egg whites.

SERVES 4 TO 6

4 cups chicken stock

½ cup thinly sliced fresh ginger

½ cup thinly sliced yellow onion

½ cup sliced scallions, plus more for garnish

½ cup sliced shiitake mushrooms

½ cup fresh or frozen peas

1 tablespoon cornstarch

Salt and freshly ground black pepper

2 large eggs, beaten

1 tablespoon soy sauce

1 teaspoon toasted sesame oil

Chili oil, for serving

1. In a medium pot, bring the stock to a light boil over high heat. Add the ginger, onion, scallions, mushrooms, and peas.

2. In a small bowl, stir the cornstarch together with 2 tablespoons water to make a slurry. Set it aside for now.

3. Season the broth with salt and pepper and return it to a boil, then reduce to a rumbling simmer. Pour the eggs around the pot in a spiral like you're making a funnel cake. Add two spoonfuls of the cornstarch slurry and give everything a swirl. Then add another spoonful of cornstarch slurry and swirl again, then leave the eggs alone so they can cook. Once they're set, less than 30 seconds, add the soy sauce and sesame oil. You can add a little more of the cornstarch slurry if you want the soup to be a little thicker.

4. Give everything one final swirl, then ladle into bowls, garnish with scallions, and serve with the chili oil on the table for everyone to add as they'd like.

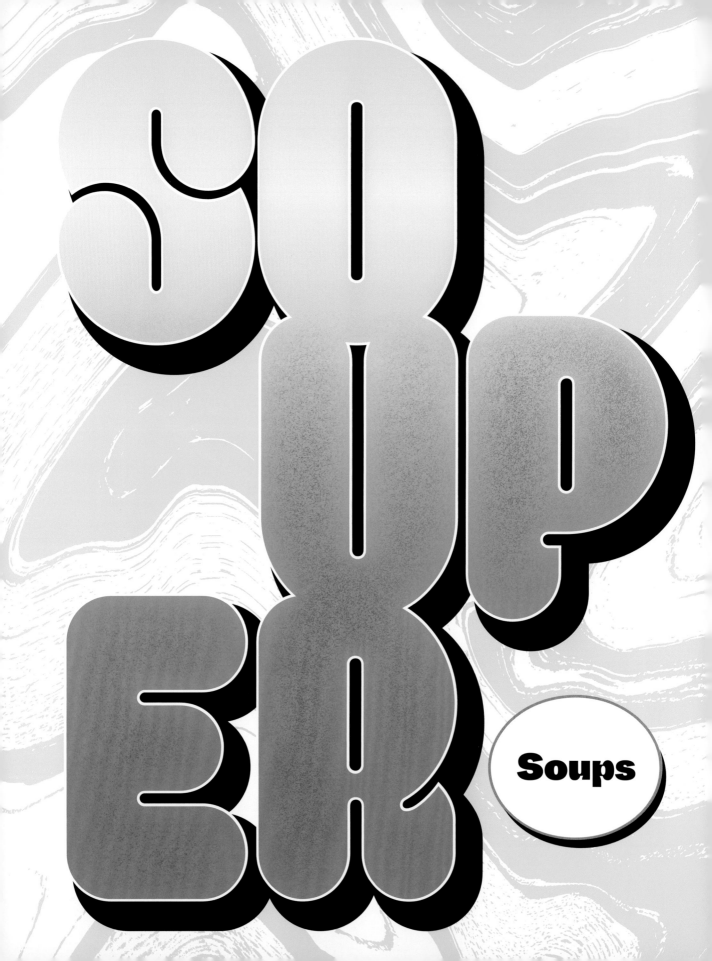

SOUP ER

Soups

The way I grew up, the kitchen always was bubbling. Alive. Kimchi fermenting on the counter, my mom's pickles burping in Country Crock tubs in the fridge, soups simmering on the stove. And when I say soups, I mean at least two pots. My mom always had at least two pots of soup or stew going on at the same time. Sometimes, she was cooking up new soups. Other times, she was making a stew in one pot and reheating last night's soup in the other, adding new vegetables to it and refreshing it with new seasonings. That was breakfast.

So, the way I cook and eat, there's always soup. Soup for every season, soup for when you're sick, soup for a party. Soup for the table, breakfast, lunch, dinner, second dinner, soups as snacks in between. You slurp some broth, you have a spoonful of rice, you grab some veggies, you gnaw on a piece of kalbi. All in one motion. And repeat.

Having a soup be present in your life all day every day is something I want to channel in this chapter. The soups here can be *part* of a meal, or they can *be* the meal, however you want to play it. These are the results of my various life experiences, but that doesn't mean you can't bring your own into it, too: All are super customizable, so you can easily swap out the fillings based on what you have.

KOREAN CHICKEN NOODLE SOUP

I was raised on samgyetang. This ginseng chicken soup is our penicillin, our superfood. Because not only does it make you feel better, it is truly medicinal and full of healing elements: In addition to the ginseng, there's also ginger, garlic, and jujubes (Chinese red dates); plus, of course, the chicken broth itself has its own restorative power. The classic way to make samgyetang is to stuff everything into the chicken, including sticky rice. I go another way and add the ingredients to the broth instead and toss in noodles instead of the rice. It's untraditional, but it's similarly restorative, I think, and follows the spirit of the tradition.

SERVES 6 TO 8, WITH PLENTY OF LEFTOVERS

1 whole chicken (4 to 5 pounds) or 2 Cornish game hens

1 ounce fresh or dried ginseng root (see Get In Where You Fit In)

2 dried jujubes, rinsed

1 star anise

2 cups whole garlic cloves (60 to 70 cloves), peeled

1 cup chopped peeled fresh ginger (about 4 ounces)

Salt and freshly ground black pepper

1 teaspoon toasted sesame oil

16 ounces somen or udon noodles

1½ to 2 cups chopped scallions

MSG (optional)

1. Place the chicken or game hens in a pot or other container, cover with water, and soak in the refrigerator for at least 2 hours. (Why? Soaking is supposed to remove the impurities from the chicken. It's also just how moms do it, so I'm not *not* going to do it.)

2. Drain the chicken or hens. In a large heavy-bottomed pot, combine the ginseng, chicken, jujubes, star anise, garlic, and ginger. Pour 4 quarts of water into the pot and set over high heat. Once it starts to boil, reduce the heat to medium-low or low. You want it at a robust simmer. Cook for 30 minutes. Taste and reseason as needed (but if it's too salty, add ¼ to ½ cup water to dilute it).

3. Continue simmering for another 30 minutes, then increase the heat and return to a boil. Add the sesame oil and noodles and cook until the noodles are done, 1 to 2 minutes, or according to the package directions.

4. Add the scallions, a bit more black pepper, and a little bit of MSG never hurts. Bring the pot out to the table and place it on a trivet. (Or, if you don't want to serve it right out of the pot, ladle the soup into a big serving bowl and bring that out the table instead.) Shred the chicken right there in the pot (or bowl) as you would carve a turkey and serve.

CHOICE WORDS: This soup, like almost every one of the soups in this chapter, makes way more than you'll eat in one sitting. I guess you can divide it to get to exactly how much you'd eat in one meal, but that'd be missing the point. These soups are *supposed* to last you all week. They're supposed to be dinner and tomorrow's breakfast. They're supposed to be foundations for entirely new dishes. That's what makes them ideal for those weeks when you know you're going to be busy, or when you're feeling low but want to cook something good and good for you that can nourish for days. These are super soups for a reason.

Bonus Round

After slurping up all the noodles in the soup, add cooked rice to your leftovers. Combine the two in a pot over medium heat and cook it down so it thickens and is almost porridge-like. Swirl a little toasted sesame oil on top and garnish with scallions if you want, maybe drop in a soft-boiled egg. That's breakfast, lunch, or dinner, or all of the above.

Get In Where You Fit In

- Fresh ginseng sometimes can be found at Korean and some Asian markets, but you also can use the dried version. If you can't find any ginseng at all, you can leave it out (it'll become a different soup—still restorative, just in a different way).

- If you're not feeling the somen or udon, try it with egg noodles or even elbow macaroni instead.

135

CREAMY ORZO CHICKEN SOUP

When I was coming up in my days as a country club resort chef, we always had a soup of the day on the menu. And a creamy soup was always a weekly standard, with good reason: It's the perfect weeknight soup that bridges the gap between a soup and a meal. It can be an appetizer, sure, but a bowl is filling and satisfying enough to be a meal on its own. I picked orzo for this, because it's also a great example of how it can step in for rice in a recipe. I also swapped out the heavy cream that's typical of creamy soups for coconut milk and added lots of vegetables in addition to the chicken and orzo. If you use precooked chicken, like a rotisserie from the market, this will be done in 30 minutes. The soup will thicken, and its flavors will deepen, the longer it sits, so don't be afraid of making enough to have leftovers.

SERVES 6 TO 8

3 tablespoons extra-virgin olive oil, plus more for drizzling

1 cup diced carrots

1 cup diced celery

1 cup diced yellow onion

2 tablespoons minced garlic

Salt and freshly ground black pepper

1 cup good enough white wine, whatever you would drink

4 tablespoons (½ stick) unsalted butter, plus more as needed

1 tablespoon all-purpose flour, plus more as needed

2 cups chopped cooked chicken

2 cups uncooked orzo

2 quarts chicken stock

1 tablespoon chopped fresh thyme

1. In a large Dutch oven or other heavy-bottomed pot, heat the oil over high heat. When the oil begins to smoke, add the carrots, celery, and onion and sauté until the onions are a touch translucent, about 2 minutes. Add the garlic, season with salt and pepper, and sauté for another minute. Tip in the wine and keep cooking until the wine is syrupy and has almost reduced completely, just over 1 minute. Add the butter.

2. Once the butter has melted, add the flour and whisk. The liquid will thicken up immediately. Reduce the heat to low, add the chicken and orzo, and pour in the stock. Increase the heat to high and bring to a boil. Reduce the heat to medium-low, add the thyme, and simmer for about 5 minutes.

3. Add the coconut milk, broccoli, and lemon juice and continue to simmer until the orzo is just about cooked, 5 to 7 minutes. Add the scallions, parsley, two splashes of Worcestershire sauce, and a handful of Parmesan. At this point, adjust the soup to where you want it to be: You may want to add a little more olive oil or lemon juice or more butter. If the broth is too thick, add a little bit of water to thin it out. If it's too thin, add a sprinkle of flour to thicken it up. If it's still too thin, combine the cornstarch with 1 tablespoon water to create a slurry. Add the slurry, a little bit at a time, to the soup until it's as thick as you'd like.

1 cup canned full-fat coconut milk

1 cup chopped (or shaved using a mandoline) broccoli florets

¼ cup fresh lemon juice, plus more as needed

1 cup minced scallions, plus more for garnish

Generous 1 cup chopped fresh parsley

Worcestershire sauce

Grated Parmesan cheese

1 tablespoon cornstarch (optional)

Crushed saltines, for garnish

Tabasco or other hot sauce, for serving

Rice crackers (optional), for serving

4. Ladle the soup into bowls and garnish with Parmesan, a drizzle of olive oil, a few cracks of black pepper, and crushed saltines. Serve with hot sauce and, if you want, some rice crackers, too.

Bonus Rounds

You have a lot of options with this soup's leftovers:

- Combine the soup with day-old bread: Cube or tear the bread into smaller pieces, toss it in some olive oil, and bake it in a 350°F oven until it's nice and crispy and toasty, about 15 minutes. Reheat the soup and add the bread.

- Turn the soup into a pot pie using frozen phyllo dough or biscuit dough. Just follow the package's instructions for baking the dough. Meanwhile, rewarm the soup and ladle into bowls. When the phyllo is done, place it on top of the bowl for a pot pie experience.

- Make it a chicken casserole: Combine bread crumbs with melted butter or olive oil. Load the leftover soup into a casserole dish and shower the bread crumbs all over. Place the dish in a 350°F oven and bake until everything's warmed through and the bread crumbs are golden and crisped, about 15 minutes.

Power Up

Replace the orzo with one or two 15-ounce cans of white beans (drain and rinse the beans first, and add to the pot when you add the coconut milk).

BOMB KHA CHOWDER

I **love the sourness** of Thai soups like tom yum and tom kha. Because it's not just sour, right? It's also bright and full of umami, and you walk away feeling invigorated every time. This recipe riffs on tom kha a bit by giving it a chowder-ish vibe with some rendered bacon before adding the classic tom kha ingredients of coconut milk and galangal. It's bomb! If you're not familiar with the more sour side of Thai and other Southeast Asian soups, this take on it might be your stepping stone into that world.

SERVES 6 TO 8

1 tablespoon plus ¼ cup extra-virgin olive oil, plus more as needed

6 ounces bacon or pancetta, diced

1 medium yellow onion, thinly sliced

1 Fresno chile, thinly sliced

2 cups minced scallions (15 to 20 scallions)

½ cup minced garlic (24 to 28 cloves)

3 tablespoons sliced fresh galangal or ginger

Salt and freshly ground black pepper

9 ounces shiitake mushrooms, stems removed, caps quartered

¼ cup Thai red curry paste

4 cups canned full-fat coconut milk

2 lemongrass stalks, smashed (see Lemongrass, page 34)

4 to 5 tablespoons fish sauce

Juice of 2 to 3 limes

1 (14-ounce) package medium or firm tofu, drained and cubed

½ head green cabbage, sliced

1 (12-ounce) jar or 1 (15-ounce) can baby corn, drained and rinsed

Crushed red pepper flakes

3 cups roughly chopped or torn fresh cilantro

Lime wedges, for serving

Oyster or saltine crackers (optional), for serving

Korean Crying Tiger Sauce (optional; page 246), for serving

1. Set a large Dutch oven or other heavy-bottomed pot over high heat and add 1 tablespoon of the olive oil. After about a minute, add the bacon and cook, stirring occasionally, until the pieces have browned, started to crisp, and the fat has rendered, about 5 minutes.

2. Add the remaining ¼ cup olive oil, the onion, chile, scallions, garlic, and galangal and sauté for about 1 minute, or until they release their aroma. Season with salt and pepper and sauté for 2 more minutes, adding more olive oil if necessary to keep things moving.

3. Add the mushrooms, then make some room at the bottom of the pot where you can add the curry paste. Toast the paste a bit before combining it with the other ingredients. Sauté until everything starts to caramelize, 3 to 4 minutes.

4. Reduce the heat to medium-low and add the coconut milk, lemongrass, and 2 cups water. Simmer for 10 minutes, then add 4 tablespoons of the fish sauce and the juice from 2 limes. Stir the pot, then add the tofu, cabbage, and baby corn. Simmer for another 8 minutes to allow everything to cook through and release their love, then begin finessing the soup to taste: Taste and add another 1 tablespoon fish sauce and the juice from another lime if you think it needs it. The broth should be loose but still viscous. If it's too thick, add ¼ cup water to thin it out. Taste again and make any other adjustments to the seasoning.

5. To serve, remove the lemongrass and galangal and discard (or compost). Ladle the soup into bowls and add a bit of pepper flakes and cilantro to each. Serve with the lime wedges. If you want, have oyster crackers and the crying tiger dipping sauce on the table.

Power Up

If you prefer, you can omit the bacon at the beginning and instead begin building the soup with the olive oil, onion, chile, scallions, garlic, and galangal.

RESET

I was an angry, angry kid for many, many years. I actually wasn't any good at being truly mean, but I was a rough and tough teen and college kid with a turtle shell exterior. At one point, I don't think I smiled for three years straight.

Then, as a young up-and-coming chef, I carried that anger with me. I was a yeller. I'm not proud of it, but I admit it. I never touched anybody or crossed a physical or sexual line, but I'd say some mean shit and that still ain't right.

In the early days of our food truck Kogi BBQ, we were roaming Los Angeles streets, making short rib tacos and kimchi quesadillas in the middle of the night for crowds that self-organized into lines on the sidewalk before we even parked.

It was in those early days that I felt no rules except mine applied. I drew up this ludicrous idea that no one could ask for any alterations or substitutions. What I was cooking was freedom, I thought. This was art. This was enlightenment. You get what you get and you don't get upset.

Ironically, though, it was me who got upset.

I truly want to apologize to anyone from 2008 to 2010 who felt my wrath if all you did was ask for the salsa on the side. If I snatched the taco out of your hand and gave you your money back midbite and closed the flap doors and peeled off, leaving you in a cloud of smoke exhaust . . . I am sorry.

Looking back, I realize that I put on a mask and spit out fire because I believed that anger was strength. It was my coping mechanism. I grew up in a tough environment, so this was my armor, and if I let it down, then I was not cool, not safe, and people could read me and fool me. I needed that anger, but really it was me who was a fool.

I was afraid to truly be myself. And my true self was someone who was much, much softer than the toughie I pretended to be. Tender, you might say. Even emo.

On the Kogi truck, my anger was fueled by ego and the immature idea that only I was right. Only I knew how you should experience those tacos that I made, because you had to feel what I felt. Only I understood the art behind the food, only I was fighting for creative freedom and respect. And if I could protect the integrity of this one thing, just this one thing out of all the things in the world, then my life finally would mean something.

That's a lot to put on a little taco. That's a lot to put on everyone around me. It was delicious, yeah, but getting mad at a guest for not eating that taco exactly how I imagined they should eat it? That's silly.

It was actually at Kogi where my armor of anger began to crack. People came through and ate a taco and saw a bit of themselves in the flavors—and, by extension, in me. They let their guard down, they told me open, vulnerable stories about themselves. No filters, no embarrassment. It was because of their honesty that I had the strength to be honest, too, about who I was: Not really a tough guy, but a sometimes dorky little boy who loves to eat and tell jokes. Someone who just wanted life to be a big endless macaroni salad that everyone could stick their hand in and scoop from, always.

And the more open everyone was, the more open I became, too. I loosened up; it didn't have to be my way or no way. I started to double down on the real me. I made friends I never would have if I hadn't let my guard down. Together, we've created culture and community filled with lots of laughter. And tons of amazing food, of course.

I'm gonna tell you the truth: It took the miracle of the Kogi truck and its phenomenon for me to step out of myself to see myself and let me be me. I was able to reset how I saw myself. I didn't realize it then, but that reset was exactly what I needed.

And that's exactly what we need sometimes, just to push that button on your third eye and allow yourself to see things from outside your body. If you're going through your own journey of feeling like it's you versus the world, hopefully my experience and this book can help draw the missing bridge for you so you don't have to rely on miracles. You are your own miracle. Button pushed.

MY
BOO
144

THE CHOI OF COOKING

Shabu shabu is one of my favorite things to eat, but it's one of those dishes where you have to appreciate its nuances, where less is going to turn into more. The broth for this starts out very simple; some may even say bland, because you sit down when it's just water coming to a boil in a pot on a tabletop burner. But as the vegetables and beef are added, the broth takes on layers of flavor. The beauty of it is that you're right there to taste the transformation as it happens since you don't have to wait for shabu shabu to be "done" in order to serve it. The whole point is to start it up when it's *not* done, when it's just water and a promise in a pot. Everyone participates in taking the vegetables from raw to cooked to dunked in ponzu sauce and enjoyed. The quantities I list below for each ingredient are just a start; you can easily add to it for a big party, and it's not a bad idea to have a little extra of each anyway, so you can keep refilling the pot until everyone's had their fill. At that point, add the noodles to end the meal. In a way, you and your family and friends take a real journey with the shabu shabu, traveling with it from one state to another to another, picking up things and becoming more complex along the way. Shabu shabu is life.

SERVES 4 OR MORE

Broth
14 ounces firm tofu, cubed

1 cup cubed (¾-inch) sweet potatoes

1 cup cubed (¾-inch) carrots

1 cup sliced zucchini

1 cup halved stemmed shiitake mushroom caps

1 cup sliced yellow onions

1 head napa cabbage, leaves chopped into 2-inch pieces

1 cup baby bok choy halves (sliced lengthwise)

¼ cup toasted sesame oil

¼ cup soy sauce

A few pinches of MSG (optional)

Salt and freshly ground black pepper

1 cup mung bean sprouts (4 ounces)

½ bunch (5 to 6 leaves) perilla or shiso leaves, stacked and sliced into ribbons

2 bunches scallions, sliced

Toasted sesame seeds

For the Table
1 pound rib-eye steak, thinly sliced

Cooked rice

Salt and freshly ground black pepper

Ginger Ponzu Sauce (page 246)

16 ounces udon noodles

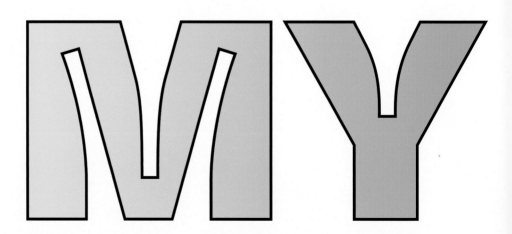

1. *Make the broth:* Set a large pot or Dutch oven on a portable burner at the table (see Stovetop Shabu Shabu). Add 3 quarts water and turn the heat to high. When it begins to gently boil, add the tofu, sweet potatoes, carrots, zucchini, mushrooms, onions, cabbage, bok choy, sesame oil, soy sauce, and the MSG if you want. Reduce the heat to medium, or just enough to keep the broth at a light rolling boil.

2. Season the broth lightly with salt and pepper (note that you'll also be dipping ingredients into the ponzu sauce, which is seasoned, too). Drop in the bean sprouts, a few perilla or shiso leaves, minced scallions, and some sesame seeds into the pot.

3. *For the table:* Place the sliced rib-eye on a platter and set it on the table. Give everyone their own bowl of rice. It's self-serve from here: Everyone should spoon some broth into their bowls and dig into the vegetables as they finish cooking. To cook the meat, pick up a slice and swish swish swish it in the broth to cook. You can adjust your own seasoning with the salt and pepper on the table. Dunk everything into the ponzu sauce before eating.

4. Right at the end, when the broth is almost empty of vegetables and meat, add the udon and finish the meal with a bowl of noodles.

STOVETOP SHABU SHABU: If you don't have a portable burner or want to make this all in one shot in one pot, make the broth as directed above but keep the bean sprouts, perilla, scallions, and sesame seeds aside. Once all the vegetables are nearly tender, 5 to 6 minutes, season the broth with salt and pepper, then add the noodles and rib-eye. Once cooked, turn off the heat and add the bean sprouts, perilla leaves, scallions, and sesame seeds. Ladle into individual bowls and serve with rice and the ponzu sauce on the side for dipping.

Get In Where You Fit In

Shabu shabu is an easy way to eat a *lot* of vegetables, and it's also a great way to clean out the fridge, so don't feel limited by what I include in mine. Add more of anything you want.

Bonus Round

After everyone's had their fill and finished off the noodles, you can combine what's left of the soup with some cooked rice to make porridge: Place the soup in a pot over high heat and add about half as much cooked rice as you have broth. Bring the broth to a roaring boil, then season with 1 tablespoon toasted sesame oil, 1 tablespoon ponzu sauce, a splash of soy sauce, a splash of fish sauce, and pinches of salt and pepper. Taste and add more of the seasoning elements as needed. Continue boiling until the broth thickens a little bit more, then turn it down to medium and add a knob of butter and any final touches, like sesame seeds, sliced perilla or shiso leaves, Thai basil, minced Thai bird's eye chiles, a drizzle of chili garlic sauce, or a soft-boiled egg, before serving.

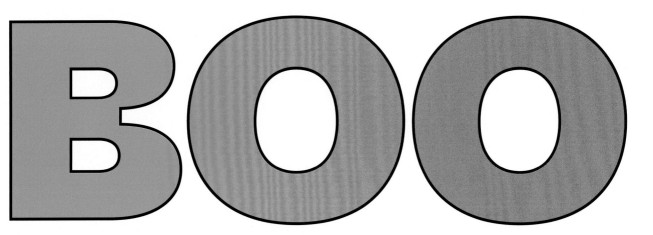

OXTAIL BRISKET SOUP

This soup is a Voltron of a soup. It combines two of my childhood dishes: sul-lungtang, a soup with ox bones and brisket, and kkorigomtang, an oxtail soup. Both of these soups are homey, family dishes that stick around for days and linger over time and become the foundation for childhood memories. As the soup simmers, the steam will permeate your whole house. After eating a bowl, you'll feel like Chapstick, moisturized inside and out.

This soup also freezes really well. It'll keep in an airtight, freezer-safe container for up to 3 months.

SERVES AT LEAST 6 FOR TODAY AND THE REST OF THE WEEK

2½ pounds oxtail (see Note)

½ pound beef tendon (see Note)

½ pound beef brisket

3 leeks, white and light-green parts only, halved and washed well

1 cup whole garlic cloves (30 to 40 cloves), peeled

3 tablespoons minced garlic

½ cup soy sauce

Salt and freshly ground black pepper

Cooked rice, for serving

Toasted sesame oil

1 bunch scallions, minced or sliced on the bias, for garnish

Toasted sesame seeds

Flaky sea salt

1. In a large pot, combine the oxtail, tendon, and brisket and pour in enough water to cover. Place the pot in the fridge and soak for at least 4 hours or overnight. (Moms do this to remove the impurities, so I do it, too.)

2. After soaking, drain and rinse the meat and the pot. Return the meat to the pot and add 4 quarts water. Bring to a boil over high heat. Reduce the heat to medium-low, partially cover the pot, and simmer for about 3 hours.

3. Cut the leeks crosswise into 2-inch pieces and add them to the pot along with the whole garlic cloves, minced garlic, and soy sauce. Season with salt and pepper.

4. Simmer, uncovered, until the oxtail, brisket, and tendon are fork-tender, 30 minutes to 1 hour. Every once in a while, check the broth to skim the fat and add more water as needed to keep the meat submerged.

5. Remove the brisket and slice it into smaller chunks, or shred it into pieces with a fork. Return it to the pot.

6. To serve, scoop some rice into a bowl. Add some oxtail, brisket, and tendon. Fill the bowl with some broth, then add a few drops of sesame oil. Garnish with scallions, sesame seeds, and flaky salt. Serve.

NOTE: You can find tendon fresh or frozen at Asian and Latino markets. Some national supermarket chains like Whole Foods may carry it, too, and your local butcher probably has tendon as well. You can often find oxtail already sliced and packed up for you in the meat department at the supermarket; if it's not cut, ask the butcher to slice the oxtail into 2- to 3-inch pieces.

CHOICE WORDS: There's a special quality about the two oxtail soups in this book. As anyone who's grown up with oxtail simmering in a broth on the stove will tell you, this is a humble cut that you can't haphazardly cook. It will take most of the day to prepare and simmer to a point where tough gives way to tender. You will have to be home to babysit it, to give it your attention and love. But what you put in will come back tenfold, because the soup will last all week and morph into different things as the days go by. It's also super nutritious: full of collagen, high in protein and iron.

Bonus Rounds

This soup unfolds into different new dishes throughout the week. With the leftovers, you can:

- Turn it into a Spicy Oxtail Yukaejang (page 148).

- Make a meat platter like a suyuk, a Korean dish of boiled meat and vegetables. Remove the meat from the soup and slice. Lay the slices on a platter or large dish. Ladle the broth into small bowls and serve with the Soy-Ginger Sauce (page 244).

- Make it a noodle soup by adding ramen noodles to the broth.

- Add cooked rice to the soup, place it over medium heat, and cook until it reduces into a porridge.

- Make fried rice. When you don't have much broth left, and just little bits of meat and vegetables remain here and there, combine all that's left with some cooked rice in a hot wok or skillet and make fried rice.

SPICY OXTAIL
YUKAEJANG

One of the ways you can use my Oxtail Brisket Soup (page 146) is to treat it as a base for another soup. That's what I do here. This is a spicy offshoot of the oxtail soup, with kimchi paste, gochugaru, scallions, and bean sprouts. Use any part of the oxtail soup that you have left, being sure to include at least some broth in addition to the solids. (If you don't have enough, you can make up the difference with beef broth. And if beef broth is all you got, use it all.) If you've had yukgaejang, the Korean spicy shredded brisket and vegetable soup, the flavors and feel of this soup is just adjacent to that.

SERVES 6 TO 8

6 cups Oxtail Brisket Soup (page 146), beef broth, or a combination of both, plus additional broth as necessary

¼ cup minced scallions

3 tablespoons Kimchi Paste (page 255)

3 tablespoons Soy-Ginger Sauce (page 244)

1 tablespoon gochugaru

1 tablespoon fish sauce

1 tablespoon toasted sesame oil

MSG

Salt and freshly ground black pepper

Handful of mung bean sprouts, rinsed

Cooked rice, for serving

1. In a medium pot, bring the oxtail soup to a simmer over medium heat. Add the scallions, kimchi paste, soy-ginger sauce, gochugaru, fish sauce, sesame oil, a few pinches of MSG, and good pinches of salt and pepper. If you want more broth, add more broth. Simmer for 10 minutes, then add the bean sprouts. Warm the sprouts in the soup for about a minute.

2. *You can serve this up one of two ways:* Each person gets their own bowl of rice with some soup ladled on top, or give everyone a rice bowl but place the soup in one big bowl to share family-style at the table.

Bonus Round

When you finish the rice (or instead of eating this soup with rice), you can turn this into a spicy noodle tomato soup. Slice 2 Roma tomatoes into wedges. After simmering the soup for 10 minutes, add the tomatoes and rice noodles or thin egg noodles. When the noodles are done, add some lime juice, fish sauce to taste, slices of jalapeño, Thai basil, cilantro sprigs, rau răm, any herbs you have, really, and serve.

MAKE It RAIN

This is a chapter full of family meals and solo nights: noodle dishes like clam pasta (page 154) that can feed you and a big group of your friends, and rice bowls that are just enough for you, your PJs, and the couch. In both dishes are a ton of vegetables and good proteins, tucked between strands of spaghetti or on top of a mound of rice.

Everything in here is designed to satisfy always, but especially when that carb craving hits. I'm no stranger to the extra-large bowls of noodles, and there was a time I could follow up a big bowl of pasta with another big bowl of pasta. But I've learned ways to satisfy that craving just by being intentional about how I plan out my meal: Try filling up on a salad plus a soup and a few vegetable or tofu appetizers first, *then* help yourself to that bowl of pasta or rice. For recipes where I call for wheat noodles, you can always use low-carb alternatives like shirataki noodles, zucchini noodles, or carrot ribbons. And feel free to reach for wild or brown rice instead of white rice whenever you like.

Whatever you put in them, these are comfort foods more than anything else. My comfort food. And now hopefully your comfort food. Nothing beats a rice bowl or a noodle bowl when you need to just be with that most tender part of yourself, whether it's after a long day at work or when you just need a moment. A moment to breathe and say fuck the world, don't bother me right now. These are those dishes that got your back.

COLD BIBIM NOODLE SALAD

I **didn't grow up** eating a bowl of lettuces and other raw greens as a meal. A little handful of cold noodles, a savory sauce, and tons of vegetables on top: Now, *that* was a salad. I'm sharing my version of a salad with you now, so you can make this part of your world of salads, too. It's a great dish to take on picnics or to work for lunch: Pack everything separately, then toss it all together when you're ready to eat (which is why we're calling this bibim noodles: *bibim* means "mixed" in Korean). Or you can do what teenagers in Korea do and have bibim noodles between work or study sessions or as an afternoon snack. A bowl of these noodles, a few small bites like kimbap and tempura, and you and your friends at 4 p.m. just talking, talking, talking like there's no tomorrow: That's the best way to eat this.

SERVES 5 OR 6

1 pound somen noodles (see Get In Where You Fit In)

1 tablespoon toasted sesame oil

1 teaspoon minced garlic

Pinch of salt

1 cup Magic Sauce (page 247)

Toppings

2 to 3 Persian (mini) cucumbers, thinly sliced

1 head romaine lettuce, shredded

1 bunch perilla leaves, thinly sliced (see Get In Where You Fit In)

1 cup chopped kimchi

Toasted sesame seeds

1. Cook the noodles according to the package directions and let cool completely.

2. Meanwhile, in a small bowl, combine the sesame oil, minced garlic, and salt. Set aside.

3. To serve, add a handful of noodles to each serving bowl and spoon about 2 tablespoons of the Magic Sauce right on top. You can add the toppings to the bowls any way you want. I place the sliced cucumbers and shredded romaine right on top of the sauce, followed by ribbons of perilla and a pile of kimchi. Finally, I very lightly drizzle the sesame oil/garlic mixture over the bowl and garnish with toasted sesame seeds all over. However you build your bowls, serve them with the rest of the Magic Sauce for the table, so anyone can add more if they want.

Get In Where You Fit In + Power Up

- Your bowl, your rules. This salad is super customizable, so depending on what you like, use more or less of any of the things I have, or throw in other vegetables like, say, raw snap peas or blanched mung bean sprouts, sliced mushrooms, or add soft-boiled eggs or tofu.

- If you can't find perilla, you can swap it out for a shiso or mint.

- Somen noodles are very thin Japanese wheat noodles. If you can't find them, you can use thin rice noodles, angel hair pasta, soba, or even udon instead.

- Use shirataki noodles, or omit the noodles altogether and outfit your bowl with even more sliced vegetables.

CLAM I
PAS

I love linguine alle vongole (linguine with clams). This version hails back to the classic, but I add a little bit of my own journey to it—specifically, Scarlett's Pasta, which we created back when I consulted on the movie *Chef.* If you remember the movie, you know the pasta: It's the aglio e olio (spaghetti with garlic and oil) that Jon Favreau's Carl makes for Scarlett Johansson's character, Molly. That recipe involves simmering the garlic in oil to deepen its flavor and bring out its sweetness to flavor the dish. I borrow that technique for this pasta; I also add a bunch of cheese, which is not usually served with seafood pastas . . . but it's good here anyway. To make this clam pasta, you'll need to create a nice steamy environment for the clams to cook, so use a shallow pan with a tight-fitting lid. If your lid is a little loose, place a piece of foil over the pan, then cover. That should help create a good seal.

SERVES 4

2 pounds Manila clams

Kosher salt

1 cup extra-virgin olive oil

12 large garlic cloves, thinly slivered

12 ounces spaghetti

1 tablespoon crushed red pepper flakes, plus more for garnish

Freshly ground black pepper

1 cup good enough white wine, one you would drink

4 to 5 tablespoons unsalted butter

Juice of 2 lemons

1 bunch fresh parsley, chopped, plus more for garnish

½ cup grated Parmesan cheese, plus more for garnish

1. Scrub the clams under running water to remove the dirt on their shells, then place them in a large bowl. Cover with cold or room temperature water and add a big pinch of salt. Leave them alone for 30 minutes to 2 hours so they'll purge their sand and grit, then pull them out of the water. Give them one more good rinse and set aside.

2. Warm a large shallow pan over medium heat. Add the olive oil and heat until it's warm, about 1 minute. Add the garlic slivers, ideally in one layer so they're completely submerged under the oil. Reduce the heat to a bare simmer. Leave the garlic until it's a deep golden brown, about 15 minutes. As it browns, occasionally swirl the oil and adjust the flame so it browns evenly. This will take some patience, but you don't want window dressing here: You don't want to bring the heat up to push it to brown faster, because you won't be cooking the inside. You want to give the garlic the time it needs to soften and caramelize. Trust me—it'll be worth it in the end.

RECIPE CONTINUES ON PAGE 156

3. Meanwhile, bring a large pot of salted water to a boil and cook the spaghetti according to the package directions. Reserving about 1 cup of pasta water, drain the pasta.

4. Increase the heat under the oil to medium. The oil will bubble a little more aggressively. Add the pepper flakes and pinches of salt and black pepper. Pour in the white wine and once it begins to boil, add the clams, give the pan a good shake, and cover. Cook until the clams open, 2 to 3 minutes. Any clams that don't open: toss.

5. Uncover and add the drained spaghetti along with the reserved pasta water. Toss to coat the pasta with the garlic oil, then cover and cook for another 30 seconds. Uncover and add 4 tablespoons of the butter. Toss well to coat. Taste and add another tablespoon of butter if you'd like, then add the lemon juice. Increase the heat to high, season with salt and pepper, add a swirl of olive oil, the parsley, and the Parmesan, and toss.

6. To serve, transfer everything to a big bowl and garnish with Parmesan and parsley.

Bonus Round

This technique of simmering the garlic under the oil until it's browned and buttery and soft and fucking delicious isn't just limited to this pasta. Make another batch of this garlic confit, cool it, put the whole thing, garlic and oil, in an airtight container, fridge it, and take it out for another bowl of pasta. Or, smash a few slices on crusty slices of bread, mash two or three slivers into butter, throw it in a vinaigrette, drizzle the oil into your instant ramen. Instant flavor.

Get In Where You Fit In

I use Manila clams here, but you can also use the same amount of littleneck clams instead.

Power Up

- If you don't want to fill up on carbs, make this pasta as just one part of a meal. The Cacio e Pepe Caesar Salad (page 98) or Tuna Salad Niçoise Bibimbap (page 92, but without the rice) would be perfect to start. Then roll out appetizers like Calabrian Chile Broccoli Rabe (page 66) or Stir-Fried Pea Shoots (page 68). *Then,* get to this bowl of noodles.

- You can swap out the noodles for shirataki or zucchini noodles, or cook up some wild rice instead.

Veggie on the LO MEIN SPAGHETTI

This one is part mall food court Chinese American stand meets the Old Spaghetti Factory, part Saturday morning cartoon. Or, that sums up how I wanted this to feel. Because it's definitely not your favorite Chinese American restaurant's lo mein, even if it might look like it from a distance. Get up close, though, and look: Where you would expect thin egg noodles you're getting thicker, larger spaghetti noodles instead. Between that and the mountain of vegetables, the plate looks super colorful and larger than life. It's playful, it's *fun*. And it's super easy to make; if you know how to make noodles, you'll know how to make this. It is *so* easy that a kid can make it, and that's no shade. Make this in the morning and eat it while you're in your superhero PJs watching Pokémon. Use as little or as much spaghetti as you'd like.

SERVES 6 TO 8

12 to 16 ounces spaghetti

2 to 3 tablespoons toasted sesame oil, plus more for serving

1 cup thin strips fresh ginger (about 3 ounces)

1 cup thinly sliced yellow onions

½ bunch scallions, cut into thin strips

2 tablespoons minced garlic

Salt and freshly ground black pepper

4 cups sliced shiitake mushroom caps (8 ounces)

3 medium carrots, cut into matchsticks

6 ribs celery, cut into matchsticks

1 medium bell pepper, thinly sliced

6 to 7 tablespoons soy sauce

2 tablespoons chili garlic sauce, sambal oelek, or sriracha

1 tablespoon unsalted butter

4 cups mung bean sprouts

MSG (optional)

1. Cook the spaghetti according to the package directions, but pull it out and drain about 1 minute before it's done cooking. Set aside.

2. Heat a large pan or wok over high heat. Add 2 tablespoons of the sesame oil, the ginger, onions, scallions, and garlic and sauté until they're aromatic, 1½ to 2 minutes. Season everything lightly with salt and more generously with pepper and toss. Stir in the mushrooms, carrots, celery, and bell pepper and another 1 tablespoon sesame oil if you need it to keep everything gliding in the wok.

3. Add the cooked spaghetti and use tongs to fold the vegetables into the noodles until everything is evenly distributed. Add 6 tablespoons of the soy sauce, ¼ cup water, the chili garlic sauce, and butter and stir. Add the bean sprouts, fold, toss, and stir to bring the sauce together and distribute the bean sprouts. Taste and add up to another tablespoon of soy sauce and a pinch of MSG if you want. Toss until the noodles have a golden brown hue from the sauce and the vegetables are tender and cooked through, another 5 to 10 minutes—basically, until it looks like spaghetti lo mein!

4. Finish with a splash of sesame oil and serve.

(Future) Sweatpants Version

To save Future You some time, you can cook the noodles in advance and refrigerate them until you're ready. You don't even need to warm up the noodles before using them; just add them cold to the wok. They'll need a minute or two to loosen up, but keep folding and they'll disentangle as they absorb the moisture from the vegetables and heat from the pan.

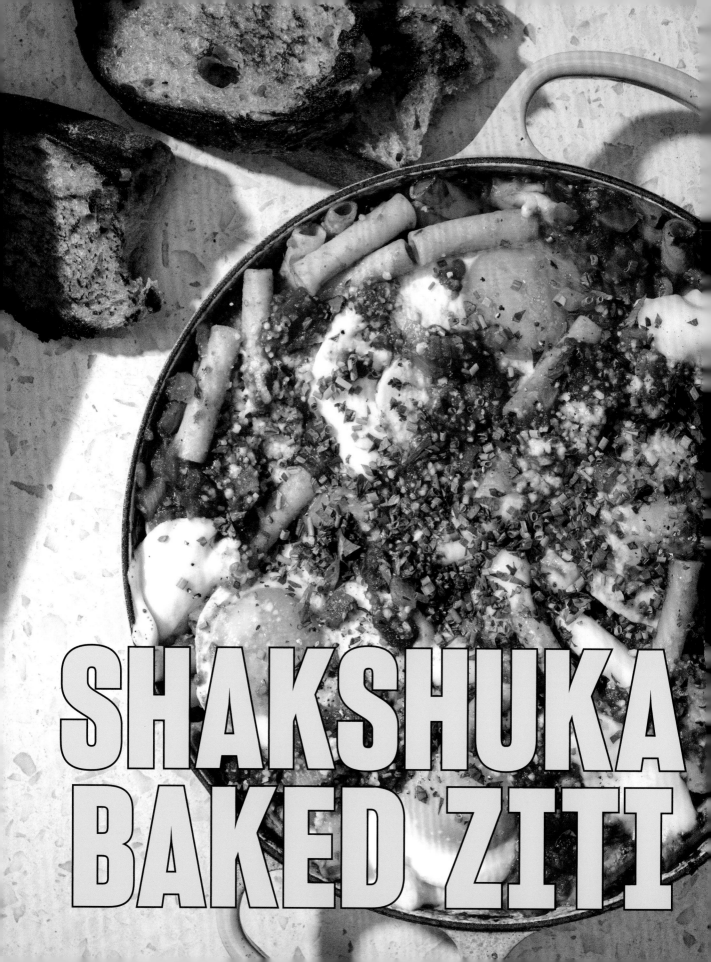

SHAKSHUKA BAKED ZITI

This dish is a hybrid of shakshuka and baked ziti, where the eggs, bell peppers, and spices in some versions of shakshuka intersect with the pasta and cheeses of baked ziti. You end up with a pretty great one-pot dish that makes plenty for a family or a group. It'll satisfy your appetite for pasta that you can round out with a few dishes—a salad, a vegetable or side or two—and it can go on the dinner table on a Tuesday night just as easily as it can be part of a weekend brunch spread.

SERVES 6

2 tablespoons extra-virgin olive oil

2 cups diced yellow onion

1 cup minced scallions

1 cup diced bell peppers (any color)

2 tablespoons minced garlic

Salt and freshly ground black pepper

½ cup white wine, whatever you would drink

2 (28-ounce) cans whole peeled tomatoes, undrained

1 tablespoon smoked or sweet paprika

1 tablespoon crushed red pepper flakes

½ tablespoon ground cumin

½ tablespoon chili powder

1 pound ziti or penne, cooked and drained

6 large eggs

6 ounces fresh mozzarella cheese, sliced

1 cup grated Parmesan cheese, plus more for garnish

Chopped fresh parsley, for garnish

Minced fresh chives, for garnish

1. Preheat the oven to 450°F.

2. In a large Dutch oven or other ovenproof heavy-bottomed pot, heat the oil over high heat. When shimmering, add the onion, scallions, bell peppers, and garlic. Season with salt and pepper. Sauté until they start to color and lightly caramelize, about 3 minutes. Pour in the white wine and deglaze, stirring with your spatula or wooden spoon to pick up all the bits on the bottom of the pot. Add the canned tomatoes with their juices, and smush the tomatoes to crush them a bit. Cook over high heat for 15 minutes to reduce and thicken the sauce.

3. Stir in the paprika, pepper flakes, cumin, and chili powder. Add the pasta and distribute it evenly in the sauce. Crack the eggs one by one into the bed of sauce. Cover and transfer to the oven to bake until the whites begin to set, about 5 minutes.

4. Uncover and add the mozzarella slices between the eggs. Shower the Parmesan all over, taking care not to completely cover the yolks. Cover and pop the pot back into the oven and bake until the whites are completely set, the yolks are semi-custardy, and the cheese has melted, 10 to 13 minutes.

5. Spoon the pasta into individual plates. Everyone should get an egg on top. Garnish with a fuck-ton of chopped parsley, chives, and more Parmesan. Serve.

Power Up

Replace some or all of the pasta with cooked white beans or chickpeas.

SOMET
IT'S JU
YOU AN
YOUR U

UNDERWEAR RICE BOWL

Lots of meals require getting everything prepped out, and I do love a dish with pretty knife cuts and shit, but sometimes it's just you and your undies or PJs and you just want to make something good and something quick so you can watch the game or catch up on that TV show. That's this. My dad taught me this one; he'd make it when my mom had to leave for the day and left us to our own devices. To this day, this bowl transports me to a safe space every time I eat it. The key here is the temperature of the rice: It has to be super, super hot so it'll cook the raw eggs you'll drop in there.

MAKES 1 BIG BOWL

3 cups very hot rice, either scooped immediately after cooking or microwaved to reheat

Good knob of unsalted butter

2 large eggs

1 tablespoon toasted sesame oil

2 to 3 tablespoons soy sauce

1 tablespoon crushed toasted sesame seeds

Furikake

Butter Kimchi Jam (page 254) or store-bought chopped kimchi

Spoon the rice into a large bowl. Add the butter to the hot rice and mix it up until all of the rice is coated with all of the butter. Crack the eggs directly into the rice and stir. The eggs should cook in the hot rice as you mix it all up (if they don't, pop the bowl into the microwave for 1 minute). Once cooked, add the sesame oil and 2 tablespoons of soy sauce. Taste and add up to another tablespoon of soy sauce if you want. Garnish with sesame seeds and sprinkle as much furikake over the bowl as you want. Add the kimchi and watch your game.

Get In Where You Fit In

You can eat this simple bowl of rice just as it is, and that would be perfect in its own way. But this bowl also is a blank slate to which you can add a bunch of vegetables and other things. A few ideas:

- If you have a bag of frozen or canned vegetables, heat it up with the rice.

- If you have some greens in the fridge, like spinach or bok choy or cabbage, drop them in boiling water until they're tender, then dunk them in iced water to stop the cooking, then add to your bowl.

- Throw in your leftovers. Of anything. It'll work.

- Sliced avocado.

- Add a fried egg, or fry the two eggs instead of cracking them into the bowl raw.

- I use soy sauce to season the bowl, but if you have some Soy-Ginger Sauce (page 244) or Magic Sauce (page 247) or any other sauce you like stashed in your fridge or pantry, you definitely can use that instead.

TAKE CARE

I've had an authority complex my whole life. Still do. As soon as someone says things should be this or that way, or you have to do this, man, I shut down. That's why I try to teach by example, or with what looks like an I-don't-give-a-fuck attitude, but really I do care a lot. I just want the message to get across without being a nagging weight. Obviously, I have to explain stuff in this book, but I am trying to use as few words as possible. What I really want you to do is to just get in there and start cooking.

If you don't cook a lot, or if you treat recipes like lifeboats, I get that you might have anxieties in the kitchen. But trust yourself to figure it out. Every time I've thrown someone into the deep end with nothing but the pan and the ingredients and the flame on high, that sink-or-swim instinct kicks in. People always figure it out. I offer some rough measurements and advice on techniques, but cooking's so immediate and visceral that most people pick it up pretty fast and self-correct along the way. I'm not saying your dish will be perfect the first time you cook with me, or even the second time. But if you intend to cook the dish as best you can, it will always be good. You will always learn something. And it always will be better the next go around.

And that's the key: intention. You have to cook with intention. Think about your happy place or a little ritual you do. Maybe you brew your coffee a certain way every morning. Or there's a method to how you organize your manga collection or sit yourself down to get ready to journal. Or there's a way you add butter to your popcorn at the movie theater, dress your hot dog, ease into your couch to relax. Whatever it is, you focus your intentions on just that thing in that moment. You're 100 percent present and accounted for.

There's a bit of selfishness in all this, and I don't mean that in a bad way. We take little bits of time for ourselves throughout the day. I want us to embrace those moments and to think of cooking as one of those times, too, when you can and should give yourself your full attention. Because if you do allow yourself to be fully absorbed in the idea of cooking, I bet it will improve three- or fourfold. Half of cooking is just being there and having the true intention to learn, to cook, to make something good. You can be funny, you can be sarcastic, you can be silly, you can be unruly as hell . . . up until the point when you actually start to cook. When you start cooking, you have to be there. You can't be negligent or careless. You're on deck, in the pocket. It doesn't matter what you're making. You have to take a real swing.

Take the onigiri (page 168). It's plum paste. It's rice. It's seaweed. That's it, right? It is. And it isn't.

It's super easy to make, but it doesn't mean you should treat it with any less care than any other dish. All the little details still matter. How are you going to cook the rice? What's your perfect ratio of filling to rice? How do you want to mold the rice in your hands? What size seaweed do you want to use to wrap it in, and how are you going to wrap it?

Maybe you'll end up cooking the rice a little too long so it's a bit mushier than you like. Maybe you'll take a bite and think, Damn, I should have added more paste. But you truly committed to the moment. You did your best. You still can be proud. It's still delicious. You can only do better next time. And everything you learned and the habits you started to form while making the onigiri are all things you'll carry forward to the next thing you make. Over time, these will stack up and make you a better cook.

This cookbook is me cooking with you. The only thing I ask is that you show up and be here. And by cooking from this book, you'll pick up what I'm putting down.

A **rice ball is** one of the most perfect snacks. It's filling in all the good ways, and it's so portable that you can take it with you anytime, anywhere. You can fill it with anything. For mine, I'm going classic and using umeboshi, a Japanese pickled plum that's sometimes used for medicinal purposes. But it doesn't taste like medicine: It's tart, cherry-like, sour, and sweet in all the good savory ways. Jars of umeboshi are available at Japanese and Korean markets. The sheets of seaweed are, too; they may be labeled as seasoned or roasted dried laver or nori. I don't have any specific measurements to give you on this one—it's all feel and pretty simple to make. But, as I say in my piece about taking care to show up and be present even for the little stuff (page 166), it doesn't mean you should treat this simply. Take a moment and focus on every component and make every component as great as you can. It'll only make you a better cook.

MAKES AS MANY AS YOU WANT

Umeboshi (pickled plum), seeds removed

Hot rice

Furikake

Pack of salted dried seaweed sheets

Soy sauce and/or hot sauce, for serving

1. Place the umeboshi in a bowl and mash it up with a fork to form a paste. In another bowl, mix the rice with a few sprinkles of furikake.

2. Spoon some rice into one hand. Scoop a little ball of umeboshi paste right in the middle. Add more rice on top and use your hands to mold the rice into a compact, squat triangle. Coat the sides with furikake. Wrap the seaweed around the rice any way you want—you could tuck the rice into the seaweed like a taco, you could place the rice in a strip of seaweed just big enough for you to grip, whatever you like. Serve with the soy sauce and/or hot sauce, and consume copious amounts.

Get In Where You Fit In

Rice balls are like mini rice bowls: blank slates. You can stuff your rice ball with anything: tofu, scrambled eggs, avocado, sashimi-grade tuna, grilled and chopped vegetables, or grilled chicken.

NIGIRI

SHRIMP
FRIED RICE

Shrimp fried rice is maybe one of the best dishes, ever. No matter where you go, it's almost always one of the best things you can order. Even the plate makes a statement on arrival: It lands like a box of jewels, with the shrimp glistening pink, the eggs hued a deep golden yellow, the scallions a brilliant emerald green. And to top it all off, everything is studded in a glittery bed of rice. I want to channel that feeling of specialness here, except as pretty as the bright-yellow strips of eggs are, I prefer to softly scramble the eggs and work them right into the rice. The eggs will enrobe the kernels and bind them together, and I find it makes for a more harmonious bowl of fried rice. Scrambling the eggs into the rice will make the bowl a little wetter than if you cooked the eggs separately, so, if you prefer, you can always beat the eggs, scramble them separately, and add them to the wok at the end of the cook. If you can, use jasmine or any other medium-grain rice for a stir-fry like this, as those varieties of rice are not as sticky as others and won't clump as much. As for the shrimp, I keep medium-sized ones whole in this recipe, but you can cut them into 1-inch pieces, or use rock shrimp.

SERVES 4 TO 6

2 tablespoons toasted sesame oil, plus more as needed

1 pound medium shrimp

Salt and freshly ground black pepper

1 tablespoon minced garlic

1 tablespoon minced scallions

6 cups day-old cooked rice, preferably jasmine

2 tablespoons soy sauce, plus more to taste

1 tablespoon unsalted butter

3 large eggs, beaten

Sliced scallions, for garnish

½ lime

Chili garlic sauce (optional), for serving

1. Heat a large wok or nonstick skillet over high heat. Once it's hot, add the sesame oil and the shrimp and season with salt and pepper. Toss the shrimp until they're nearly cooked through and opaque, about 1 minute 30 seconds. Remove the shrimp and set aside.

2. Add a touch more sesame oil to the wok. Toss in the garlic and scallions, season with salt and pepper, and sauté until they're aromatic, about 30 seconds. Add all of the rice and spread it out at the bottom of the wok. Leave it untouched for about 1 minute to brown ever so slightly, then toss toss toss for 2 minutes. Add the soy sauce and toss again, scraping the bottom of the wok to make sure you get all the little bits of garlic and scallions that may be stuck there. Stir-fry for about 1 minute.

3. Make a little space in the pan and add the butter. Once it's melted, add the beaten eggs, season with a small pinch of salt and pepper, and softly scramble the eggs. Once the eggs are mostly set but not yet completely cooked through—they should still be a bit loose—begin to stir them into the rice.

4. Add the shrimp, reduce the heat to medium-low, and toss everything to work in the eggs. Taste and add a touch of soy sauce if you want, plus lots of cracked black pepper. Keep stirring until the shrimp and eggs are cooked through and the rice is a little crispy and fluffy and there aren't any more bits of uncooked egg, 5 to 7 minutes. Taste and adjust the seasoning.

5. Transfer the fried rice to individual rice bowls or one big bowl with a big spoon to serve family-style. Garnish with sliced scallions and finish it with a squeeze of lime. If you want, pass chili garlic sauce at the table.

NON NAAN
FLATBREAD

This is a delicious flatbread that has the flavor of a scallion pancake, like the ones you find at 101 Noodle Express in the San Gabriel Valley (about 10 miles east of downtown Los Angeles) and other Chinese restaurants, but eats more like a naan. The best thing is, these are quick and easy to make. They're also real fun to have right out of the pan, while they're still hot and have all their crisp. You also can wrap or roll it around some grilled vegetables or leftover shredded meat like oxtail from Oxtail Brisket Soup (page 146). I include a dipping sauce here, but if you already have the Soy-Ginger Sauce (page 244) ready to go, you can use that instead.

MAKES 8 FLATBREADS

2 cups all-purpose flour

1 cup rice flour

1 overflowing cup minced scallions, plus some for garnish if you want

1 teaspoon garlic powder

1 teaspoon toasted sesame oil, plus more for cooking the breads

Salt

1 cup boiling water

Unsalted butter

Chili Sawse (recipe follows), for serving

1. In a large bowl, mix together the all-purpose flour, rice flour, scallions, garlic powder, sesame oil, and a pinch of salt. Add the boiling water and combine it with the flour to make a dough. Transfer the dough to a lightly floured surface, and knead it until it comes together, then round it into a ball or fat disc.

2. Set aside the dough and reflour your work surface. Divide the dough into 8 equal portions, and roll each portion into a small ball. Flour your rolling pin and place it in the middle of a ball of dough. Roll up, then down. Rotate the dough 90 degrees and roll up, then down again. Keep rotating and rolling until it's about 6 inches in diameter. It doesn't have to be a perfect round. It can be a rustic 6 inches. As you roll, it will become very thin and more and more delicate, so try to make quick, firm motions.

3. In a medium skillet set over medium heat, add just enough sesame oil to coat the bottom of the pan, plus a tablespoon or so of butter. When the butter starts to froth, add the dough and cook until it starts to blister and the edges begin to crisp, about 3 minutes. Lightly season the surface of the dough with salt and flip. Cook this side until it blisters and colors, too, 2 to 3 minutes. Take it off the pan and, ideally, eat immediately with the Chili Sawse. Repeat with the remaining dough.

4. To plate it, spoon some sauce over the flatbread and garnish with a sprinkle of scallions. Serve the rest of the sauce on the side.

Chili Sawse

MAKES ABOUT 1¼ CUPS

½ cup soy sauce

½ cup rice vinegar

2 tablespoons toasted sesame oil

1 tablespoon chopped fresh cilantro

1 tablespoon chili crisp

1 tablespoon chili garlic sauce

1 teaspoon sriracha sauce

½ teaspoon minced garlic

½ teaspoon minced Thai bird's eye chile

½ teaspoon minced fresh ginger

Minced scallions or a piece of a carrot, minced

In a medium bowl, combine the soy sauce, vinegar, sesame oil, cilantro, chili crisp, chili garlic sauce, sriracha, garlic, chile, and ginger. Stir to combine, then add some scallions or carrots. Set aside, or place in a jar or other container, cover, and refrigerate until ready to use.

CHOICE WORDS: This recipe originally started out as a proper scallion pancake. In my head, I was going to make a pancake as flaky and layered as the best croissant, with tons of green onion flavor. But I couldn't get it to work. I got real frustrated and mad at myself. Then I relaxed. I took a breath. Instead of trying to force it, I let myself experiment and go outside the path of tradition. And that's how I got here, to a flatbread that's absolutely not a scallion pancake or a naan, but hits both feelings. And that's a big part of *The Choi of Cooking*: letting yourself make mistakes, letting go of preconceived ideas so you can have room to adapt, and finding side doors to your destination.

The **CHEEZY WEEZY**

This riff on the grilled cheese sandwich tastes like how I cook: sweet, savory, spicy, confusing, bomb. It's embedded in my DNA, actually, because it's rooted in the Kogi BBQ truck; if you've been to Kogi, you'll recognize this as a version of a special called The Cheezy Weezy. This one has four different types of cheeses—Gruyère, yellow and white cheddars, and Parmesan—for some complexity; they also melt at different temperatures, which gives you some fun textures as you bite into it. And while this is a grilled cheese sandwich, the real stars are the sliced bananas right down the middle. Finding them there is a surprise, like when you find a rice cake in your kimchi stew. They bring Kogi's rugged, wild freedom to the sandwich while giving it a kiss of sweetness, too. When you need comfort by way of a sandwich, this is the one to make.

MAKES 4 SANDWICHES

Extra-virgin olive oil

Unsalted butter, at room temperature

8 slices sourdough or white sandwich bread

2 ounces Gruyère, shaved or thinly sliced, or 4 slices provolone cheese

4 slices yellow cheddar cheese

4 slices white cheddar cheese

1 to 2 bananas, sliced

¼ to ½ cup Sweet Chile o' Mine Sauce (recipe follows)

2 ounces Parmesan cheese, shaved or thinly sliced

1. Place a griddle or medium skillet over medium-high heat and drizzle in a bit of olive oil.

2. Butter one side of each slice of bread. Once the griddle is nice and hot, make 1 sandwich by adding 2 slices butter-side down to the griddle. You should hear a bit of sizzle.

3. Pile some Gruyère, a slice of yellow cheddar, and a slice of white cheddar cheese onto one of the bread slices. Shingle a few slices of banana on the cheddar cheese, then spread a heaping tablespoon of sweet chili sauce right on top. Top with some Parmesan cheese and close the sandwich with the other slice of bread. Keep cooking until the bread is golden brown and crisp, 2 to 3 minutes. Lightly re-butter the top slice of untoasted bread, then carefully flip the sandwich and cook until that slice is crisp and golden brown, another 2 to 3 minutes. Remove the sandwich from the pan and serve immediately. Then make the remaining sandwiches. Enjoy!

Get In Where You Fit In

If you prefer, you can turn this into a Monte Cristo (without the meat). Place some flour in a bowl or plate. In a separate bowl or plate, beat 3 eggs. Get your skillet going over medium heat. Coat the sandwich in the flour, then dip both sides in the eggs. When the skillet's hot, add a pat of butter and toast the bread until it's golden brown, then flip and repeat.

Power Up
- Use whole-grain rather than sourdough or white bread.
- Make the sandwich with just one type of cheddar and halve the amount of the other cheeses.

RECIPE CONTINUES ON PAGE 176

Sweet Chile o' Mine Sauce

I make a lot of my sauces from scratch . . . but this isn't one of them. Not exactly. In fact, I like this sauce because it *isn't* totally made from scratch, and it shows how you can build on, and be creative with, something that's already out there. In this case, I take a bottle of Thai sweet chili sauce from the market, add a bunch of aromatics and citrus to it, and end up with a new chili sauce that also spreads like a savory marmalade. I use Mae Ploy's Sweet Chili Sauce, which is available at many supermarket chains, but use what you like and adjust to taste. We have a version of this sauce at Kogi, and people drench everything in it: their burritos, their tacos, their sliders. Everything. It'll be good on The Cheezy Wheezy (page 174) and other sandwiches and eggs, too. Like I said. Everything.

MAKES 3 CUPS

5 whole garlic cloves, peeled

1 serrano pepper, stemmed

½ small yellow onion

1 cup fresh Thai basil

1 cup store-bought Thai sweet chili sauce

¼ cup minced scallions

¼ cup fresh lime juice

¼ cup orange juice

3 tablespoons chopped fresh cilantro

2 tablespoons fresh lemon juice

1 tablespoon gochugaru

1 tablespoon chopped fresh ginger

1 tablespoon toasted sesame seeds

1 tablespoon sriracha

Pinch each of salt and freshly ground black pepper

In a blender, combine all of the ingredients plus 1 tablespoon water and puree until smooth. It's ready to use as soon as you make it. Store leftovers in a jar or other covered container in the refrigerator for up to 1 week.

Bonus Rounds

A few other ideas for how you can use this sauce:

- Add it to a peanut butter and jelly sandwich.

- Brush the sauce on top of a glazed donut for an inside-out jelly donut.

- Spoon some into your oatmeal.

- Spread it on your bagel.

- Mix it into a bowl of rice.

- Serve it with satays and other grilled meats.

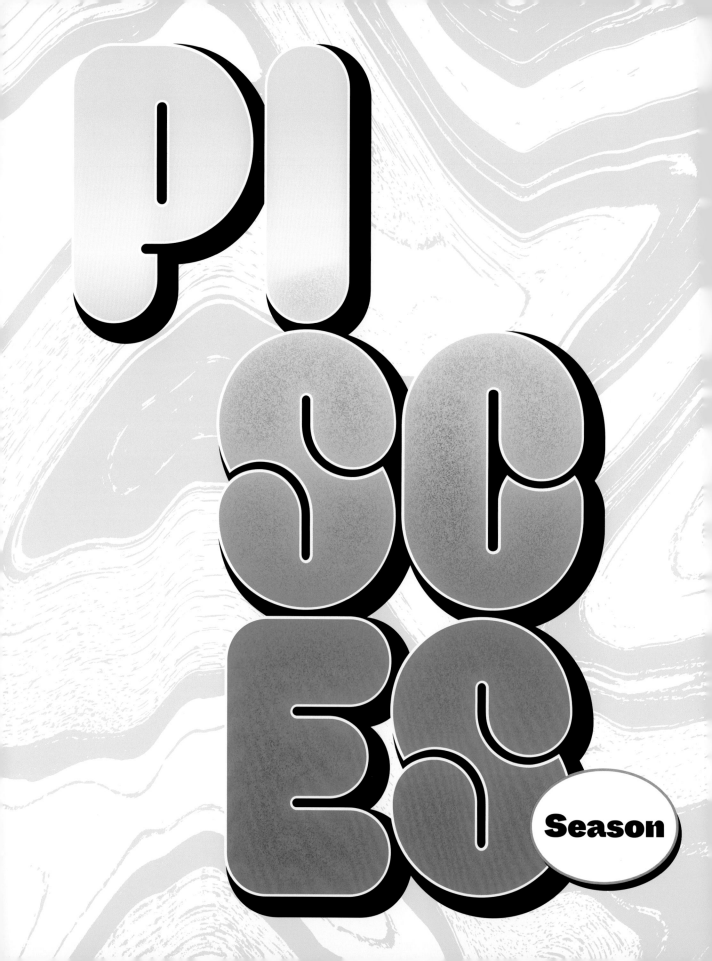

PISCES

Season

Seafood was a huge part of my mom's cooking. She and my dad would spend the weekends scouring all of southern California for the freshest fish and shellfish, so something like a small, whole grilled fish was a very usual part of our spread of banchan and other dishes. But I realize not everyone had a childhood like mine, and if that's the case for you, the idea of cooking seafood at home can be intimidating, something best left to restaurants. And I get that: Fish and shellfish don't have a huge margin for error and will go from not cooked to overcooked in a nanosecond.

But if you're willing, learning how to make the recipes in this chapter will reward you with dishes that are good, good for you, and good to go in less than an hour. Start with the Yuzu Aguachile (page 180) to get the hang of bringing fish home, then maybe try the Hawaiian-Style Garlic Shrimp (page 194). Then, the next you know, you're going to be grilling a whole fish (page 188) on your own. And at any point, if you mess up and overcook something? That's okay! It'll probably be good enough. Put it in a rice bowl with some salsa (pages 250 and 251), or the Soy-Ginger Sauce (page 244), or the Magic Sauce (page 247). Part of the cooking journey—and a big part of my philosophy—is being generous with yourself, embracing imperfection, adapting and readapting, getting back up, and trying again next time.

YUZU AGUACHILE

I love aguachile. It's such a refreshing, light, filling way to enjoy fresh seafood, and while I haven't yet been to aguachile's hometown in Sinaloa, Mexico, I have real fond memories of the aguachiles made with fresh Gulf shrimp during my times in Rosarito and Ensenada. The classic way to make aguachile is to cure the shrimp and fish in a mix of chiles, lime juice, and water. For a different flavor profile, I use yuzu juice and yuzu koshō (a fermented paste that is made of the peels of yuzu, chiles, and salt) instead of the lime. Both are available at Japanese markets; some Asian markets will have them, too. This is my homage to the classic.

SERVES 4

Sauce

¼ cup whole garlic cloves (7 to 10 cloves), peeled

½ medium yellow onion

Extra-virgin olive oil

1 jalapeño, roughly chopped

1 serrano pepper, roughly chopped

10 ounces tomatillos, husked, rinsed, and chopped

½ bunch fresh cilantro, roughly chopped

½ cup yuzu juice

1 heaping tablespoon green yuzu koshō

Salt and freshly ground black pepper

Assembly

1 pound sashimi-grade yellowtail or scallops, sliced

Minced or sliced fresh chives, for garnish

Flaky sea salt

Extra-virgin olive oil

1. *Make the sauce:* Set aside 3 of the smaller garlic cloves. Place the rest of the garlic in a medium skillet, preferably cast-iron. Add the onion. Coat the cloves and onion in a bit of olive oil. Set the pan over medium heat and toast the garlic cloves just until they're lightly browned on all sides. As you do so, rotate the onion a few times so it chars on all sides. Once the garlic toasts and the onion chars, remove and cool. Chop the onion.

2. In a blender, combine the toasted garlic, the 3 reserved raw cloves, the onion, jalapeño, serrano, tomatillos, cilantro, yuzu juice, yuzu koshō, and fat pinches of salt and pepper and puree on high for 1 minute.

3. Transfer half of the sauce to a bowl. Strain the remaining sauce through a sieve into a separate bowl.

4. *Assemble the dish:* Spoon the unstrained sauce onto a large plate or shallow bowl. Fan out the fish right on top, then spoon the strained sauce over the fish. Garnish with chives, flaky salt, and a swirl of olive oil.

CHOICE WORDS: Acids bring dishes alive. You've probably noticed by now that I use acids a lot in my cooking. The aguachile sauce here is full of them: the yuzu juice, yuzu koshō, and even the tomatillos have an acidity to them. Acids make you feel light. They make you feel balanced. They're the smear of mustard on a pretzel, the finishing touch. All in all, they're great ways to punch up a dish and give it some kinetic energy. Next time you feel like your dish could use something to take it to the next level, take a look at your acids. The difference between a pretty good dish and a pretty great one can be as simple as a squeeze of lime.

Sweatpants Version

Instead of the sashimi-grade fish, you can use frozen precooked shrimp instead. Thaw out the shrimp, place as many as you want in an ice-cold glass, and put the aguachile right in. Eat with a big spoon.

KIMCHI TUNA MELT BOATS

A tuna melt might be one of my favorite sandwiches. It has a special place in my heart because it was one of the first sandwiches I perfected when I was a young chef at a golf country club in the desert. There wasn't a secret to it; it was just paying attention to the little details: buttering and toasting every inch of the bread so its entire surface browned and toasted, not just the middle part. Making sure the tuna mixture was really warmed through so you wouldn't bite into a random cold spot. Truly melting the cheese, not half-melting it, not kinda melting it, but truly melting it. So now, how do you replicate the feel of that sandwich without the bread? Well, I thought: What if we spice it up with kimchi, crunchy celery, and a ton of scallions and eat it with crisp lettuce leaves? Bingo. These kimchi tuna melt boats hit that same feeling, I think. Note there's some mayo in here to bind everything together; I suggest you start with just a few spoonfuls, then taste and add more until it's where you like it. Honestly, that goes for the rest of the ingredients. I do include some measurements, but you really could just grab everything and make this tuna melt entirely by feel, just by tasting as you put everything together. Even then, remember, all the little things still matter. Choose crisp lettuce leaves so you get that satisfying crunch. Warm through the tuna properly. And don't rush it: Really melt that cheese. This ain't a burger or a sandwich with a bun, but it's the next closest thing—so close you won't even miss the bread.

SERVES 2

2 (5-ounce) cans tuna, drained

Mayonnaise

2 cups minced celery

1 cup minced scallions

Salt and freshly ground black pepper

Extra-virgin olive oil

½ lemon

1½ cups chopped kimchi, plus more for serving

2 tablespoons unsalted butter

2 tablespoons toasted sesame seeds, crushed

4 slices cheddar cheese

½ head iceberg lettuce, leaves separated

1. In a bowl, mix the tuna with a few spoonfuls of mayonnaise, the celery, scallions, a pinch of salt and pepper, a splash of olive oil, and a squeeze of lemon (watch out for the seeds). Taste and add more mayo if you want, or adjust the seasoning. Set aside.

2. In a medium skillet, combine the kimchi, butter, sesame seeds, and a crack of pepper. Sauté over medium-high heat until the kimchi is nice and caramelized, just a few minutes. Add the tuna mixture and warm through until everything is gloppy in a good way. Add the cheese right on top.

3. When the cheese is melted just enough, scoop the mixture into the lettuce leaves and enjoy with more kimchi on the side.

COOKING BY FEEL

I only measured shit for this book because they asked me to. The reality is, you could mess up a lot in this book, add more, add less, use different shit, but whatever you do, it'll still be delicious. This whole book can be cooked by feel. I'm just trying to get you into the mode of cooking, because cooking is a muscle; to do it well, you need practice. And you need practice not just to learn techniques and hone your skill, but to figure out what you like. You need to practice how to taste and have an opinion about what you're tasting.

Very often when we cook—especially as beginners—we just don't trust ourselves. And the more we don't trust ourselves, the more we look to other people and internalize their preferred flavors and seasonings, what they think tastes good, what they think tastes bad. But other than respecting dietary restrictions and allergies, we'd all be stuck in a stalemate if all we did was to cook to please everyone. There's a point where you have to shut everyone out and believe that if you like something, others will, too. And the only way to do that is to keep tasting. Learn what you think is sweet, what's salty. Learn what's too sweet or too salty. Make note of what stops you in your tracks, the flavor combinations that make you turn your head. Season things to a point where you say, *Fuck!*

Then have the confidence to say, *This is good* and trust that others will say *Fuck!* too.

My recipes here will give you enough technique and guidelines to get you there. Learn the recipes by making them a few times, then trust yourself enough to let go of the guardrails, breathe, and riff on them. In that way, I'm trying to teach you some advanced cooking principles about building your own flavor. But for beginners—and I say beginners not as an insult or as a judgment about your skills or aptitude, but as a way to give you permission to reset after learning my recipes so you can start again and make them your own—it's leaning into Yoda. It's leaning into the power of unlearning what you have learned, so you're not stuck in what people say about the "right" way to cook. It's about feeling and trusting what tastes good to you even if you can't explain why it tastes good to you. It's flow and letting things flow.

The Choi of Cooking is a groove as much as it is a cookbook. But, you gotta tap into that first. And that's what I'm trying to share with you. 5-6-7-8, let's dance!

The Unfried Fish Taco

PSSTCADO

I love fish tacos. When I was a teenager, I woke up on a beach in Rosarito, hungover, girl gone, a horse licking my face. Then I stumbled into a spot with fish tacos, and it recalibrated my soul. I noticed the texture and subtle flavors of the fish in every single bite. A great fish taco will do that to you; it'll force you to stop and give it your full attention. Hopefully this fish taco will make you stop and pay attention, too. This is grilled (not batter-fried) for that summer bod. But be sure to oil both the fish and the grill grates very well to prevent the fish from sticking. If you don't have a grill, you can cook this in a skillet on the stovetop instead, and the same rule applies: Oil everything well.

MAKES 8 TO 10 TACOS

Slaw
½ head red cabbage, shredded

½ head green cabbage, shredded

1 medium red onion, thinly sliced

2 bunches fresh cilantro, chopped

Extra-virgin olive oil

A few limes, halved

Salt and freshly ground black pepper

Fish Tacos
1 pound firm white fish fillet (such as snapper, cod, mahi mahi, sea bass, or swordfish), skinned

Extra-virgin olive oil

Salt and freshly ground black pepper

Stack of street taco-sized (4½ inches) flour tortillas

Pico de Gallo (page 251)

Salsa Verde (page 250)

Kewpie mayonnaise or crema

Crumbled Cotija cheese

1. Preheat a grill to medium.

2. *While the grill heats, make the slaw:* In a large bowl, combine both cabbages, the onion, cilantro, a little drizzle of olive oil, and a good squeeze from half a lime (the lime should really come through, so add more lime juice if it doesn't). Season with salt and pepper and toss. Taste, adjust the seasoning, and set aside.

3. *Prepare the fish:* Smother the fish in extra-virgin olive oil and season it well with salt and pepper.

4. Oil the grill grates. When the oil begins to smoke, add the fish. Leave it untouched for 3 to 4 minutes, or until it's about halfway cooked (you'll know because the fish will go from translucent and a little pinkish to opaque and white), then gently and carefully flip. Cook it until it's just about cooked through and flakes easily with a fork, 3 to 4 minutes longer.

5. While the fish cooks, place a few tortillas on the grill just to warm them through and make them pliable, 20 to 30 seconds, flipping them once or twice. (If you're cooking the fish on your stovetop, you can warm the tortillas in a separate medium or large skillet set on another burner.)

6. Once the fish is cooked through, place it on your work surface and use a fork to shred it into large chunks.

7. To assemble a taco, place a few pieces of fish on a warmed tortilla, then top with the slaw, pico de gallo, salsa verde, and Kewpie. Right before serving, garnish with the Cotija.

GRILLED WHOLE FISH

with Magic Sauce

If you're used to seeing and eating fish fillets, working with a larger whole fish, eyes and all, can seem a little intimidating. But whole fish is one of the best ways to enjoy fish. Since we're keeping the bones, the fish retains a lot of its moisture and flavor, and with eating the whole fish, there's little waste. Plus, a whole fish charred with grill marks on a bed of bright green herbs? You can't beat that presentation.

For grilling specifically, I like to use a branzino because it's a good size. It's big enough to serve a group but not so big that you can't handle it yourself on the grill. If branzino isn't available, another round fish, like snapper or sea bass, is great, too. I keep the flavors for the fish simple, which for me means thin slices of lemon and as many bunches of herbs as can be stuffed into the cavity of the fish. These will permeate and perfume the branzino from the inside out as it grills.

And lastly, some advice: When it comes to grilling the fish, there's always a great fear that the delicate skin of the fish will stick to the grates or the grill pan. And I won't lie, there's always a danger that you're going to end up with a hot mess. But oil the grates and the fish well, and you should get a crispy skin that will release beautifully. And if you would rather steam the fish instead, see Steamed Whole Fish with Magic Sauce (page 190).

SERVES 3 OR 4

½ cup thinly sliced cabbage

½ cup thinly sliced romaine lettuce

¼ cup thinly sliced yellow onion

Salt and freshly ground black pepper

1 whole branzino, snapper, or sea bass (about 2 pounds), gutted and scaled (see Note)

1 lemon

4 to 5 bunches fresh Thai basil

4 to 5 bunches fresh cilantro

Extra-virgin olive oil or spray oil, for the grill grates

The Orange Bang Vinaigrette (page 104) or Dijon Balsamic Vinaigrette (page 102)

Magic Sauce (page 247) or Ginger Ponzu Sauce (page 246)

RECIPE CONTINUES ON PAGE 190

1. Preheat a grill to medium-high.

2. As the grill preheats, in a medium bowl, combine the cabbage, lettuce, and onion. Season with a pinch of salt and pepper and toss. Taste, adjust the seasoning, then set the slaw aside (don't dress it just yet).

3. With gentle, caring hands, pat the fish completely dry with paper towels, inside and out. With a sharp knife held at a 45-degree angle, slash the fish a few times across the body. This will help you evenly season the fish, and it'll help the fish cook evenly, too.

4. Season the fish very generously and evenly with salt and pepper, starting with the inside cavity, then moving to the outside. Be sure you get some seasoning into the slashes, too.

5. Halve the lemon and slice one half into thin slices. Shingle however many slices as will fit in a single layer inside the fish, then stuff 2 or 3 bunches each of Thai basil and cilantro right on top of the lemon slices.

6. Generously oil the grill grates. When the oil begins to smoke, brush or spray oil on one side of the fish and place it, oiled-side down, onto the grill. It'll start to smoke and crackle right away. Grill until nice grill marks appear, 6 to 8 minutes. Oil or spray the top of the fish and flip it as cleanly as you can (two spatulas, or a spatula and a spoon will help). Cook this other side, reducing the heat a touch or moving the fish to a cooler spot on the grill if you hear the fish crackling a little bit too much, until that side is crispy and the fish is cooked through, 4 to 6 more minutes.

7. Take all the herbs you have left and place them on a serving platter. Make them look comfortable and soft. Place the remaining lemon slices all over, cutting a few more slices from the other half of the lemon if you'd like.

8. When the fish is done, flip it over onto a plate (you flip the fish over so the side you just spent a good few minutes making crispy doesn't steam and get soggy). Slide the fish right onto the bed of herbs.

9. Take the slaw you set aside earlier and toss it with a few spoonfuls of the vinaigrette. Taste and add more dressing if you think it needs it. Give it one final toss.

10. Bring the slaw, the Magic Sauce, and the fish all out to the table and dig in.

NOTE: If you haven't shopped for whole fish before, a few tips for your trip to the seafood department: When you're there, follow your nose. It might seem counterintuitive, but most seafood really shouldn't smell that fishy. Fresh fish have clear eyes, shiny skin, and if you can see them, pinkish gills. And ask the seafood counter to scale and gut the fish for you.

STEAMED WHOLE FISH WITH MAGIC SAUCE: If you prefer not to grill the fish, you can steam it if you have a big enough steamer or a big enough pot and a rack or steam basket. You'll lose the crispy skin, but the steamed fish still will make people go *ooh* and *ahhh* when you bring it out to the table. After stuffing the fish with the lemon slices and herbs, place it on a heatproof plate or platter that will fit inside the steamer. Fill the steamer or pot with a few inches of water, put the basket or rack on top (make sure it doesn't touch the water). Bring the water to a boil, then carefully place the fish inside the basket or on the rack. Cover and steam until the fish is opaque and cooked through, 10 to 15 minutes. Transfer the fish to the bed of herbs and serve it with the sauce and slaw.

Get In Where You Fit In

If you don't have Thai basil or cilantro, any other fresh herbs you do have will work here, including chives, parsley, oregano, tarragon, makrut lime leaves, and thyme. If you don't have any fresh herbs, there's nothing wrong with using just the slices of lemon.

TURMERIC-STEAMED MUSSELS

These mussels are a cross between pub-style mussels steamed in wine or beer and Thai-style mussels steamed in coconut milk. I outfit the broth with tons and tons of shallots, garlic, lemongrass, and chiles so it's super aromatic. There are a bunch of herbs in here, too, including rau răm, a grassy, warming herb you'll find in Southeast Asian and many Asian markets. Serve the mussels with some steamed rice or thick slices of crusty bread just like you'd have at an alehouse, or both!

SERVES 2 OR 3

3 tablespoons extra-virgin olive oil

½ cup minced shallots

½ cup minced garlic (24 to 28 cloves)

½ cup minced lemongrass (from about 8 stalks; see Lemongrass, page 34)

½ cup minced Fresno chiles or jalapeños

Salt and freshly ground black pepper

1 pound mussels, scrubbed and debearded

½ cup good enough white wine, whatever you would drink

1 cup canned full-fat coconut milk

Fistful of rau răm (see Get In Where You Fit In)

1 tablespoon ground turmeric

¼ cup fresh lime juice

2 tablespoons unsalted butter

1 tablespoon fish sauce

1 tablespoon chili garlic sauce or sambal oelek

½ bunch fresh cilantro, chopped, for garnish

1. In a medium or large sauté pan or skillet with a lid, heat the olive oil over high heat. When it begins to shimmer, add the aromatics: the shallots, garlic, lemongrass, and chiles. Season with salt and pepper. Sauté until aromatic, 2 to 3 minutes.

2. Add the mussels, season with salt and pepper, and stir. Pour in the wine and scrape up any caramelized bits of anything stuck to the bottom of the pan with a wooden spoon or spatula. Reduce the wine by about half, then shake the pan and add the coconut milk and rau răm. Cover and steam the mussels until they open, 3 to 4 minutes. Uncover and discard any mussels that are still closed.

3. Add the turmeric, lime juice, butter, fish sauce, and chili garlic sauce. Transfer to a large serving bowl and garnish with the cilantro before serving.

Get In Where You Fit In

- If you can't find rau răm, feel free to swap it out for mint or lemon verbena.

- If you don't like mussels, swap them out for clams, shrimp, or even scallops.

CRISPY. SALMON. LEMON.

A salmon fillet with a skin so crisp it practically shatters is one of the most satisfying, and quickest, meals you can make on a Tuesday night. But I get it. Just the possibility of that skin sticking to the pan so you have to spend the rest of the night scraping it off when you got work the next morning doesn't sound like a risk you want to take. Still, one night, give this a try. The key here is to make sure the fish is dry so the skin can really crisp up. And if all you did was make salmon with a crispy skin, that'd be pretty good, but the butter lemon sauce you make right in the pan is what helps this go from pretty good to pretty damn good. If I had a lemonade stand, I'd sell this sauce.

SERVES 4

Extra-virgin olive oil

4 skin-on salmon fillets
(4 ounces each) or 1 pound
skin-on salmon, cut into
4 portions

Salt and freshly ground black
pepper

2 tablespoons unsalted butter

Grated zest and juice of 1 lemon

Chimichurri (page 247) or Garlic
Herbed Butter (page 244)

1. Place a large sauté pan over medium-low heat and add a glug of olive oil.

2. While the pan heats, check if your salmon fillets are completely dry. If not, pat them dry with a paper towel, then season them with salt and pepper and smother the fillets with olive oil.

3. When the oil in the pan begins to shimmer, carefully place the salmon skin-side down. It'll start to crackle and pop. Sear until the skin is crispy and the fillets release from the pan, 4 to 5 minutes, depending on how thick or thin your fillets are.

4. Flip, add the butter and swirl the pan to melt it. Add the lemon zest and juice to the butter and spoon some over the fillets to glaze them. Cook just until the salmon is light pink and cooked through, 2 to 3 minutes longer.

5. Move the salmon from the pan to plates, skin-side up to show it off. Spoon some chimichurri or place a pat of herbed butter right on top. Pass the rest of the sauce or butter in a small bowl at the table.

Hawaiian-
Style
Garlic

SHRIMP

The first time I had Hawaiian-style garlic shrimp was, like everybody else, at one of the shrimp trucks that line the North Shore on the island of Oahu. And whether you order from Giovanni's or Romy's or any other truck, it always feels like a what-the-fuck moment when you get a plate. It's shrimp tossed in a ton of garlic and a ton of butter, and somehow those things feel like a revelation when you're there. There's something really beautiful about shrimp-truck shrimp, and I wanted to re-create that at home so you can cook it yourself rather than going out when the mood strikes. It's a pretty easy cook, which makes it perfect for those times when you just don't have the energy to do much: Just toss the shrimp in a garlic marinade in the morning and when you're hungry, it'll cook up in less than 5 minutes. Use any size shrimp you want. You also can use rock shrimp. I include a bit of mochiko (sweet rice flour) in the marinade, which gives the shrimp some body and will help crisp them up, but if you don't have any, you can use all-purpose flour instead. Eat this up as they do on the North Shore: with two scoops of rice and a wedge of lemon.

SERVES 4

1 pound shell-on shrimp, deveined

½ cup minced garlic (24 to 28 cloves)

½ cup soy sauce

½ cup chili garlic sauce

½ cup extra-virgin olive oil, plus more for searing the shrimp

1 tablespoon mochiko (sweet rice flour)

Salt and freshly ground black pepper

4 tablespoons unsalted butter

Minced fresh chives

1 lemon, halved, seeds removed

Cooked rice, for serving

1. In a large bowl, combine the shrimp, garlic, soy sauce, chili garlic sauce, olive oil, mochiko, and pinches of salt and pepper. Cover with plastic wrap, place in the fridge, and marinate for at least 30 minutes, or you can go as long as overnight. The longer in the marinade, the better it'll be.

2. In a large pan, heat 1 tablespoon olive oil over high heat. When it begins to shimmer, use tongs to pull half of the shrimp directly out of the marinade and into the pan, or as many shrimp as you can fit in a single layer without overcrowding. Sear the shrimp until they're charred and just start to turn opaque, 1 to 2 minutes. Flip, sear the other side, and cook until the shrimp are almost cooked through and not quite completely opaque, about 30 seconds. Transfer to a large plate.

RECIPE CONTINUES ON PAGE 196

3. Add a touch more oil to the pan, then add the remaining shrimp, again in a single layer. Sear and cook until the shrimp begin to turn opaque, 1 to 2 minutes, then flip. Once you flip the shrimp, add ½ cup of the marinade, ½ cup water, and the butter, shaking the pan to emulsify and smooth the sauce. The sauce should be pretty loose, loose enough to drip off the back of a spoon. Taste and adjust the seasoning if necessary. If it's too salty, add a splash of water.

4. Remove the pan from the heat and add the shrimp you cooked earlier and toss to combine everything with the sauce. Shower the pan with the minced chives and squeeze half a lemon all over. Give the pan one more good shake.

5. To serve, distribute the shrimp among four plates. Add 2 scoops of rice onto each plate. Slice the other half of the lemon into wedges and make sure every plate gets a wedge of lemon. Serve it up.

Sweatpants Version

The longer the shrimp sit in the marinade, the longer they will have to absorb the flavors and the better it will be. If you're pressed though, you can marinate the shrimp for as little as 30 minutes. It won't be as deeply flavorful, but it'll still be good.

Bonus Rounds

Any sauce remaining in the pan is awesome brushed on a few pieces of toast. Broil the toast for a few minutes for a shrimp-y garlic bread.

Power Up

For a less buttery, less saucy version of this garlic shrimp, broil the shrimp instead of cooking it in the pan. About 10 minutes before cooking, preheat the broiler. As it preheats, melt 2 tablespoons butter and line a sheet pan with parchment paper. Pull the shrimp from the marinade and place them on the sheet pan in a single layer. Broil the shrimp 2 to 3 minutes per side until cooked through. Once the shrimp are cooked, toss them with the melted butter and chives, squeeze a bit of lemon all over, and serve.

THERE'S SOMETHING REALLY BEAUTIFUL ABOUT SHRIMP-TRUCK SHRIMP

CRAB QUAKES

These are crab **"quakes"** because we're out here in California and because they're so good, you'll shake! Take care when you make them, though; they're a little delicate because I intentionally use just enough breading to keep the cakes together, and no more. Delicate doesn't mean difficult, though; you just have to pay attention and be present. It's the little things here you have to watch out for: You want big chunks of crab in a crab cake, but if you overhandle or are too rough and tumble when combining the mix, the meat will fall apart. You also want to be real gentle when you form them into patties; if you compact them too much, you'll end up with dense crab cakes. Take some care and they'll take care of you. Don't forget to save a few perilla leaves for serving: They're not just garnish. They're great wrappers for the crab cakes.

MAKES 6 TO 8 CRAB CAKES

10 to 12 perilla or shiso leaves

1 pound lump crabmeat, picked over

1 large egg

¼ cup mayonnaise

¼ cup whole-grain Dijon mustard

¼ cup panko bread crumbs

2 tablespoons chopped fresh chives

2 tablespoons chopped scallions

2 tablespoons chopped Fresno chiles or jalapeños

1 tablespoon fresh lemon juice

1 tablespoon Tabasco sauce

1 tablespoon Worcestershire sauce

Extra-virgin olive oil

Lemon wedges, for serving

Old School Green Goddess (page 105), for serving

1. Chop a few perilla leaves until you get about 2 tablespoons. Add them to a large bowl, along with the crabmeat, egg, mayonnaise, mustard, panko, chives, scallions, chiles, lemon juice, Tabasco, and Worcestershire sauce. Ever so gently combine.

2. Still with soft, light hands, form the mixture into 6 to 8 patties about 3 ounces (a generous ¼ cup) each and as wide as the palm of your hand. Place on a large plate and refrigerate the crab cakes for 30 minutes to firm up.

3. In a large skillet, heat about 1 tablespoon oil over medium-low heat. When it begins to shimmer, add as many crab cakes as you can without overcrowding the pan. Cook until a pretty golden brown, 6 to 7 minutes. Flip and cook the other side to golden brown, 4 to 5 minutes. Repeat with the remaining crab cakes, adding more oil between batches.

4. Serve the crab cakes with the rest of the perilla leaves, lemon wedges, and Green Goddess dressing. You can take a forkful and dunk it into the dressing, or tuck a little bit of a crab cake inside a perilla leaf, spoon a little bit of dressing on top, squeeze the lemon on top, and enjoy.

Sweatpants Versions

- Refrigerating the formed crab cakes will firm them up, which will make them easier to cook. But, if you want to make the cakes sooner, you can skip that step and start cooking as soon as you form the patties. Just be extra gentle when sliding the crab cakes into the pan, and when flipping them.

- Alternatively, you can form the crab cakes today and cook 'em tomorrow: Form the crab cakes, place them on a baking sheet, and cover the sheet tightly with plastic wrap, or stack them in an airtight container with sheets of wax or parchment paper between the patties to keep them separated. Then, when you're hungry in your sweatpants tomorrow, take them out of the fridge and cook.

MEAT ME HERE

This chapter is a paradox. It's filled with meaty dishes like chicken nuggets, Taiwanese-style pork chops, a rib-eye basted in butter . . . but I hope that by the end of it, you'll eat a little less meat than you did before. In this chapter, we're going to shift, one shuffle at a time. We're going to play with proportions so we eat less meat and more vegetables—without noticing the change in ratio, without feeling like you've sacrificed or lost something to get there.

We are omnivores, but that doesn't mean we need to be inconsiderate assholes. If we're going to eat meat, let's honor the animal by not wasting its life: Use every part that you buy, don't waste it. Think about the animal's life as you honor it by cooking it with love and intention. Thank it. If you can, buy humanely raised or ethically raised meat. And let's eat less of it to hopefully preserve one life at a time. Let's prioritize flavor over portion size by infusing the meat with so many bright acids and punchy herbs and umami'd sauces that you can eat less and feel more than satisfied. And in some cases, taking down the portion size opens up space for another dish—like a salad or side of delicious vegetables.

Remember what I said in the first chapter, when we started with Vegetables? *So what I got here are ways for you to eat more vegetables without even realizing you're eating more vegetables.* That's how we end, too. Full circle. These are the final tracks that will take you back to where we all began.

Green Bean and Chicken

STIR-FRY

If you're not already incorporating vegetables into your every day, one of the easiest ways to ease into it is to start slow. Take this stir-fry: I intentionally set this up to let you decide how much chicken and green beans you want to use. Then, the next time you make it, cook it with a little less chicken and more green beans than you did before, and so on until one day, you'll wonder what it would be like to swap out some of the chicken for diced firm tofu. No matter what you do, it'll be a perfectly saucy stir-fry that can be eaten like a rice bowl for those nights it's just you and the couch, or placed on a big platter and served family-style. And you'll be on a new path with new cooking tools. You do you to make a new you.

SERVES 6 TO 8

1 to 1½ pounds green beans, trimmed

14 to 16 ounces boneless, skinless chicken, preferably dark meat, chopped into pieces the size of what you would get at Panda Express

1 heaping tablespoon cornstarch

Salt and freshly ground black pepper

2 tablespoons toasted sesame oil, plus more as needed

2 tablespoons minced fresh ginger

2 tablespoons minced garlic

2 tablespoons sliced scallions, plus more for garnish

1 cup Sweet Garlic Teriyaki Sauce (page 248)

1 tablespoon chili garlic sauce, sambal oelek, or sriracha

1 tablespoon fresh lime juice

1 generous tablespoon unsalted butter

2 heaping tablespoons chopped fresh cilantro

Toasted sesame seeds, for garnish

Cooked rice, for serving

1. Cut the green beans into halves or thirds, depending on how long they are. Set aside.

2. In a large bowl, toss the chicken with the cornstarch. Season with salt and pepper and toss again.

3. Heat a large wok or skillet over high heat. Add the sesame oil, ginger, garlic, and scallions and sauté, shaking the pan, until they release their aroma, 15 to 30 seconds. Add the chicken and sauté, adding more sesame oil as needed to keep things moving around smoothly, until the pieces are nicely browned on all sides, 3 to 5 minutes.

4. Add the green beans, season with a pinch of salt and pepper, and sauté until they're seared and maybe even a little charred, 2 to 3 minutes. Add ¼ cup water, the teriyaki sauce, and chili garlic sauce. Cook until the chicken is just about done, there are a thousand little bubbles bursting all around the edges of the sauce, and the sauce itself has reduced, thickened slightly (not syrupy), and is viscous, about 5 minutes.

5. Add the lime juice and butter. Stir in the cilantro. Garnish with sesame seeds and more scallions.

6. Serve over a bowl of rice, or transfer it all to a large bowl and serve it family-style at the table.

Get In Where You Fit In

This recipe is super versatile. Instead of chicken, dice some medium or firm tofu. Or, substitute the chicken and green beans for other proteins and vegetables; try it, for example with beef and broccoli.

COOKING FOOD FAST

You can make the Green Bean and Chicken Stir-Fry (page 202) in 30 minutes if you already have the Sweet Garlic Teriyaki Sauce (page 248) prepped in the fridge and ready to go. If you don't, you'll just need to spend a little bit of extra time making it. But if you're really pressed and don't have that time, there are plenty of other things in this book that you can cook up on any busy weeknight (page 258).

But if you got the time: Make the damn sauce. Let me tell you why.

Sometimes, particularly when you're a young cook, there's this misunderstanding about what it looks like for "real" cooks to cook. I'm talking about that image of someone, head down, picking herbs, tweezers nearby. Perfectly cut blue tape lined up and ready to be labeled. Busy with lots of finishing steps to plate up the dish. That image of the plate making its way around the kitchen for a legion of hands to add their flourishes and the chef's final intricate steps to complete the dish. All over a cascade of minutes. Yes, this is cooking—a specific kind of "high-level" way of cooking, the *Yes, chef!* way of cooking, the type of cooking that we think is sexy and demands our respect. In many cases, this image is what draws us into food.

But as I've grown older and understand cooking more, I'm realizing that a lot of what I grew up on, and what I'm connecting to now, all have something in common: They're dishes where the flavors are prepped and built over slow, solid procedures that make it possible for a dish to be cooked and served in seconds. Think a bowl of pho, a platter of Korean BBQ short ribs, a plate of tacos. This kind of food takes seconds to put together, so it seems simple. And because it seems simple, it's dismissed as food that's slapped together, or it's relegated to cheap eats lists while the hunchbacks in chef's whites get the genius moniker.

But behind the scenes of the pho that hit your table 30 seconds after you ordered it are cooks who nursed the broth and built its flavor over 18 hours. The KBBQ short ribs marinated for 12 hours, and the kimchi that's always served on the side took weeks to ferment. And yeah, it took a taquero 10 seconds to plate up three tacos, but it took hours to marinate and pile the al pastor on the spit, and a crew spent hours slicing, chopping, and blending the salsas.

My mom built flavor over time in the same way. She'd spend hours making marinades, sauces, dips, ferments, then stashing them so it'd be faster for her to cook later that week.

Blending, chopping, fermenting, prepping over hours so a dish can be served in seconds: That's what it looks like for real cooks to cook, too. And yes, it takes a good chunk of time to prepare it all, but when it's go time, you can feed yourself and your family and friends in no time. And those end up being the dishes you crave. Now, that's fucking genius.

The chef I've become is the result of a slow metamorphosis from watching my mom cook to becoming a chef at all levels of restaurant cooking to plugging into the streets with the Kogi BBQ truck to right now, right back to where I began at home, making homestyle food but with a world of experience. Putting it all together in the dishes in this book is the result of that journey, like Frodo coming back from the fires of Mordor forever changed. That's the teriyaki sauce, and that's why it's worth making even on a weeknight to make a stir-fry. Because like all my other flavor agents (pages 242 to 255), even if it costs you some time to make now, it's going to save you even more time later. You'll net positive. And the results will be deep and intricate. This isn't simple food. It's life food—and life is never simple.

SOY-GARLIC BBQ BAKED CHICKEN WINGS

This is my version of Korean-style fried soy-ginger wings. But instead of frying, we're going to do something easier: We're going to bake the wings and baste them with a glaze to give the wings their crispiness. The goal is to give you really munchable, bomb-ass wings that you can take to any party and satisfy any wing craving. If you have an air fryer, you can always air-fry these instead. And if you want these spicy, add the chili garlic sauce to the marinade.

MAKES ABOUT 24 PIECES

3 to 4 pounds chicken wings, drumettes and flats split

Sweet Garlic Teriyaki Sauce (page 248)

3 tablespoons chili garlic sauce or sambal oelek (optional)

Flaky sea salt

Toasted sesame seeds, for garnish

2 bunches scallions, sliced

1. Place the wings in a shallow baking pan, or split them among a few double-bagged resealable bags. Measure out ½ cup of the teriyaki sauce and set aside (you'll need it for basting later). If you're going for the heat, add the chili garlic sauce to the rest of the marinade and give it a stir, then pour over the wings. Place the wings in the fridge and marinate for at least 2 hours, or overnight. Refrigerate the marinade you've set aside for basting, too.

2. About 1 hour before you plan to make the wings, preheat the oven to 375°F.

3. Place wire racks on two baking sheets. Remove the wings from the marinade and divide them between the wire racks (discard the marinade). Bake the wings for 20 minutes.

4. Baste both sides of the wings with the reserved marinade and bake until they're cooked through and the skins are crispy and crackly, 20 to 25 minutes longer.

5. Remove them from the oven and glaze them one more time with the sauce. Finish with a sprinkle of flaky salt, sesame seeds, and scallions and wing it!

CHICKEN NUGGS

If you have a craving for fried chicken, well, this is a recipe for fried chicken, but nugget-sized. It's for those times when you need the crunch that only a fry can give. In those moments, it'd be better and much more satisfying to fry 'em yourself than to get the fast-food version. If you have an air fryer, you can air-fry these instead (see Power Up). Either way, the key to this fry is the few hours the chicken spends in a milk marinade, which tenderizes the pieces.

SERVES 4 TO 6

1 pound boneless, skinless chicken thighs

Salt and freshly ground black pepper

2 cups whole milk

1 cup all-purpose flour

2 large eggs, beaten

1 cup panko bread crumbs

2 to 3 cups neutral oil, like corn oil or vegetable oil, for frying

Any sauce or dip you like, such as Creamy Blue Cheese Dressing (page 107), Lemon Ranch Dressing (page 106), ketchup, or honey mustard

1. Cut the chicken into little nugget-sized pieces. Season with salt and pepper. Place them in a resealable plastic bag, bowl, or some other clean container. Pour the milk over the chicken, making sure the pieces are completely submerged. Place the chicken in the fridge and marinate overnight.

2. *When you're ready to fry, prepare a breading station:* Place the flour, eggs, and panko on three separate plates or shallow dishes, in that order. Season each with salt and pepper.

3. Remove the chicken from the fridge and transfer the pieces directly from the marinade to the flour. Coat the nuggets well, then dip them into the eggs, then roll them in the panko. Press the panko firmly into the nuggets; you really want the crumbs to stick.

4. Preheat the oven to 300°F.

5. Place a wire rack on a sheet pan and place it next to your stove. Pour ¾ to 1 inch of oil into a large heavy-bottomed pot or a cast-iron skillet and heat over high heat until a bit of panko sizzles when dropped in.

6. Working in batches so you don't crowd the pan, add the chicken to the hot oil. You want nice, steady, big bubbles all around the nuggets; if you see lots of tiny bubbles, your oil probably is too hot, so reduce the heat. Fry the chicken until a bright golden brown, 3 to 5 minutes depending on the size of the pieces. Flip and fry the other side, another 3 to 5 minutes, until the chicken is cooked through and crispy. Transfer the chicken to the wire rack to drain and cool. If all but the largest pieces are done cooking, remove the cooked pieces and pop the uncooked ones into the 300°F oven for a few minutes to finish cooking, just so you don't burn them in the pan.

7. Serve with the dipping sauce(s).

Sweatpants Version

An overnight marinade is ideal, but you can soak the chicken for just 2 hours in the marinade if you can't wait.

Power Up

If you'd rather not deep-fry, you can air-fry the chicken instead. Preheat the air fryer to 400°F. Spray the nuggets with olive or avocado oil and place them in the fryer basket, doing just a batch at a time so they're not crowded in the basket. Cook 5 to 6 minutes, flip, then cook for another 5 to 6 minutes until they're cooked through and crispy.

Braised Spicy Korean

CHICK

Originally, this recipe involved making a bunch of different sauces from scratch, then combining them into one super sauce to braise the chicken with some potatoes and veggies. It was the kind of recipe that existed before there were formal recipes, when the way to cook was passed down from generation to generation, from kitchen to kitchen, and everyone added a little something to it each step of the way. For our times, I wanted to take a different approach to get to the same place, with just one sauce loaded with multiple points of flavor, from spicy to sweet to savory to umami, a bit similar to the Korean chicken braise called dakdoritang. Before making the sauce, you'll sear the chicken piece by piece; it'll take a little bit of time, but there's no cheat code for this, no good way to shortcut the process. So, take the time to sear all the pieces right and your investment will pay off with tons of flavor added into the braise. I use dried vermicelli noodles here, but japchae (glass) noodles also are great.

SERVES 6 TO 8

Sauce

1½ jalapeños

½ cup chopped scallions

½ kiwi, peeled

½ small or medium Asian pear, peeled and chopped

½ cup maple syrup

½ cup whole garlic cloves (15 to 20 cloves), peeled

1 tablespoon minced fresh ginger

1 cup soy sauce

1 cup gochujang

¼ cup fish sauce

1 tablespoon oyster sauce

½ cup granulated sugar

½ cup gochugaru

1½ tablespoons light brown sugar

Chicken

1 whole chicken (4 to 5 pounds), cut into 8 to 10 serving pieces (2 thighs, 2 drumsticks, 2 wings, and 2 breasts, halved horizontally if especially thick)

Salt and freshly ground black pepper

½ cup extra-virgin olive oil

3 cups chicken stock

8 ounces fingerling potatoes, quartered and soaked in cold water

1 large carrot, thinly sliced

1 medium bell pepper (any color), thinly sliced

1 medium yellow onion, thinly sliced

4 to 6 jalapeños, thinly sliced

1 bunch scallions (6 to 8 scallions), cut into thirds

16 ounces dried thin vermicelli noodles

6 tablespoons cold unsalted butter

For Serving

Cooked rice

1. *Make the sauce:* In a blender, combine the jalapeños, scallions, kiwi, Asian pear, maple syrup, garlic, ginger, soy sauce, gochujang, fish sauce, oyster sauce, granulated sugar, gochugaru, and brown sugar and blend until smooth. Set aside.

2. *Prepare the chicken:* Season both sides of each chicken part with salt and pepper.

3. In a large Dutch oven or pot, heat the oil over medium-high heat. When it begins to shimmer, add the chicken skin-side down, just a few pieces at a time (otherwise, you'll crowd the pot and the pieces won't sear). Sear the pieces until they're golden brown, 2 to 3 minutes, then flip and sear the other sides, 2 minutes more. Place the chicken in a bowl or plate and repeat with the rest of the chicken pieces.

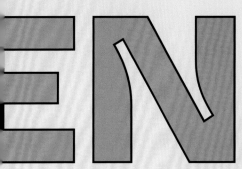

RECIPE CONTINUES ON PAGE 212

4. Once seared, fit the chicken pieces, plus their collected juices, snugly into the pot. Add the sauce and stock and bring to a boil. Reduce to medium-low, cover, and simmer for 30 minutes.

5. Add the potatoes and simmer for 10 minutes. Add the sliced carrot, bell pepper, onion, and jalapeños and cook until the carrots are soft but still a bit firm, another 10 minutes.

6. Add the scallions and vermicelli and cook until the noodles are tender, about 3 minutes. Add the butter and taste: If the broth is too thick or tastes too concentrated, add a little water to thin it out.

7. *To serve:* Scoop some rice in a bowl. Add a bit of every part of the pot—some of the sauce, a piece of chicken, some noodles, potatoes, and vegetables—on top and dig in.

(Future) Sweatpants Version

When you're making the sauce, you can easily double it and freeze half. And a few months from now, the Future You in sweatpants will thank the Present You for taking the time to double this up.

Bonus Rounds

After finishing the chicken, vegetables, and noodles, you may have some braising sauce left in the pot. If so, there a few things you can do with it:

- Make another meal by using it to braise some more chicken, or another protein like tofu or squid.

- Use it as a dip (try it with the Steamed Pork Belly, page 218)!

BLACK PEPPER TAIWANESE-STYLE PORK CHOPS

Taiwanese-style pork chop over rice is one of my favorite favorite things to eat. Compared to other types of fried chops, it's pretty tame; the coating isn't super heavy, and there aren't a lot of different flavors screaming for attention. The one thing you do taste is umami and a pronounced saltiness, and that is the point: It's meant to be part of a spread, balanced with a simple bowl of steamed rice, some vegetables, maybe with some pickles or Maggi seasoning on the side. So, if you serve these chops as one dish out of many, they can easily be split to feed a party of four (otherwise, if you aren't pulling together a spread, you may want to keep one chop all for yourself). My version here is more pepper- than salt-forward, but there is some soy sauce in the egg wash for a combo bump of salty and umami. With this much flavor in each bite, you don't need that much of a chop to feel satisfied. And while many versions of Taiwanese pork chops are coated just in potato starch, I use panko and a cloud of flour to help achieve that crisp. But be careful: It should be a very light coating, lighter than how you would bread, say, a katsu or a schnitzel.

MAKES 2 CHOPS; SERVES 2 TO 4

½ cup all-purpose flour

1 large egg

1 tablespoon soy sauce

½ cup panko bread crumbs

Salt and freshly ground black pepper

2 boneless pork loin chops (4 ounces each), pounded about ¼ inch thick

1 cup neutral oil, like corn or vegetable oil, for shallow-frying (to air-fry, see Power Up)

Cooked rice, for serving

Quickles (optional; page 52), for serving

Maggi seasoning (optional), for serving

1. Place the flour on a plate or in a shallow baking pan. Beat the egg with the soy sauce and pour the mixture onto a plate or shallow baking pan and place it next to the flour. Finally, shake the panko out onto its own plate or baking pan. Season the flour, egg mixture, and panko with salt and *plenty* of pepper.

2. Completely dry the pork chops with a few paper towels and season them with salt and pepper, too. Place a chop in the flour. Lightly flour both sides, then dip it into the egg mixture, then gently place it in the panko and coat the chop lightly. Firmly press the panko into both sides of the chop; you want it to really stick. Dust the pork with just a little bit more flour (you know how you spray perfume in the air and walk through it? That's the kind of dusting I mean: just that little bit of flour). Set aside. Repeat the breading with the other chop.

3. Set a wire rack in a sheet pan and have it near the stovetop. Pour ¾ to 1 inch of oil into a large skillet, preferably cast-iron, and place over medium heat. Wait 2 minutes, then dip a little bit of the chop in the oil. If it sizzles right away, the oil is hot enough and you can carefully slide in the chop. If not, wait another minute, then check again.

4. Shallow-fry the chop until it's golden brown and crisp, 2 to 3 minutes. Flip and fry the other side till it's golden brown and cooked through, another 2 to 3 minutes. Place the pork on the wire rack and shallow-fry the second chop.

5. Serve the chops with rice and, if desired, Quickles (and any other dishes; see Power Up) and a bottle of Maggi on the table.

Power Up

- To air-fry these chops: Preheat an air fryer to 400°F. After coating the pork with panko, spray both sides generously with avocado or olive oil, and spray the fryer basket, too. Place the chops in the basket and air-fry until the top of the chops are lightly golden brown, 7 to 9 minutes, then flip and cook until the chops are cooked through and crisped, 5 to 7 minutes. Note that if your air fryer basket is too small for both chops, you'll need to cook them separately.

- Balance the chops with a warm bowl of rice or green salad, tofu (page 114), some crudités (page 56) or Quickles (page 52), and a plate of vegetables like Stir-Fried Pea Shoots (page 68), Calabrian Chile Broccoli Rabe (page 66), or Hot Chow Chow (page 72).

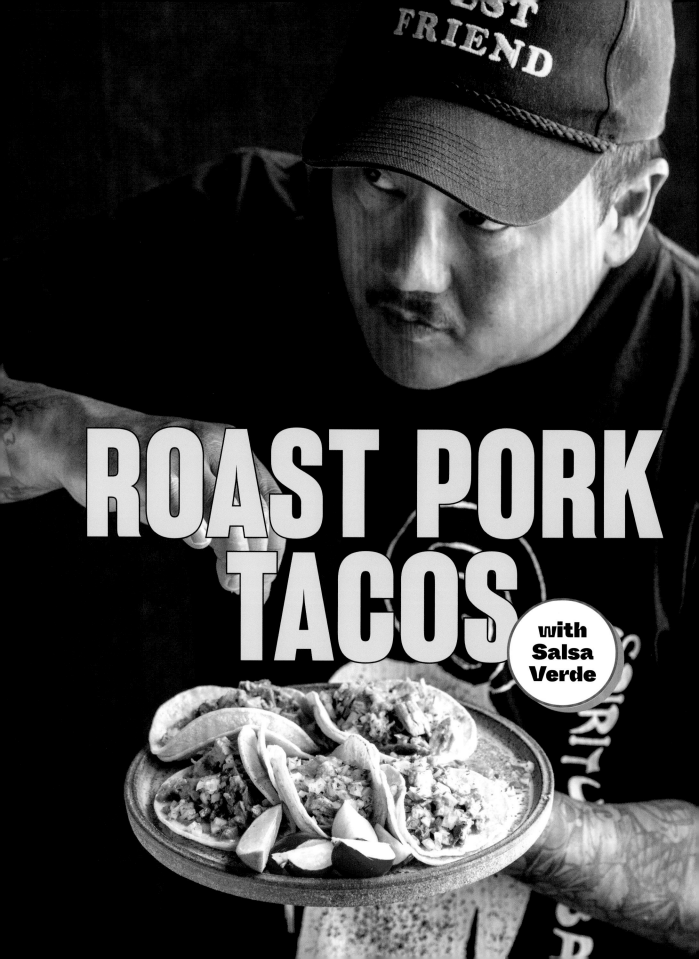

ROAST PORK TACOS

with Salsa Verde

This is a pork taco that I keep lean by leaning into the pork's own juices and fat. Rather than roasting the shoulder in a liquid that would add extra fat or sugar (or both), the pork goes into the oven dry. As it cooks, it'll release its juices and its fat will render, essentially braising the pork for us. The flavors we would otherwise build in the braising liquid are instead going to be shifted to the toppings, the cilantro-onion relish and salsa. Start the pork in the early afternoon and it'll be tender and succulent—and lean—by dinnertime. You can assemble the tacos before serving, but for a taco night, it's fun to bring everything out separately so everyone can make their own.

SERVES 6 TO 8

Roast Pork
3 pounds boneless pork shoulder, preferably a thick, stubby cut

Salt and freshly ground black pepper

¼ cup extra-virgin olive oil

4 whole garlic cloves, peeled

½ bunch fresh cilantro

Handful of thyme sprigs

Cilantro-Onion Relish
½ medium yellow onion, finely chopped

¼ to ½ cup fresh cilantro, finely chopped

1 tablespoon fresh lime juice

Salt and freshly ground black pepper

Tacos
Extra-virgin olive oil

Stack of street taco–sized (4½ inches) corn tortillas

3 red radishes, trimmed and quartered, for serving

A few limes, cut into wedges

Salsa Verde (page 250)

1. Preheat the oven to 250°F.

2. *Roast the pork:* Generously season the pork shoulder with salt and pepper on all sides, making sure to get the seasoning into all the little nooks and crannies. Drizzle the olive oil over the pork and use your hands to coat it with the oil. Place the pork, fat-side up, into a large Dutch oven or other ovenproof pot with a tight-fitting lid (you also can stack a few sheets of foil and use that to seal the pot). Add the garlic cloves right on top of the pork. Cover and place in the oven. Roast for 2½ hours.

3. Uncover and add the cilantro and thyme sprigs. Increase the oven temperature to 400°F, put the lid back on, and roast until the fat has rendered at the bottom of the pot and the pork is tender, about 1 more hour.

4. Remove the pork from the oven and let it rest for 30 minutes, covered.

5. *Make the cilantro-onion relish:* In a medium bowl, combine the onion, ¼ cup of the cilantro, and the lime juice. Give it a stir to combine everything, then season with salt and pepper. Taste and add up to another ¼ cup of the cilantro if you'd like.

6. *Make the tacos:* Uncover the pot and discard the cilantro and thyme. Remove the pork and shred or chop it into bite-sized pieces. Return the pork to the Dutch oven and toss it with all the delicious juices and the garlic in the pot, then place everything in a large serving bowl.

7. Set a large skillet or griddle over low heat and add a touch of oil. Add a tortilla and cook until it's slightly charred, about 30 seconds, then flip. When that side blisters, another 30 seconds, remove, stack, and nestle into a kitchen towel to keep warm. Repeat with the other tortillas.

8. Gather everything up and bring it all to the table: the warm tortillas, the pork, cilantro-onion relish, radishes, lime wedges, and salsa. Build your own taco!

Power Up
Instead of making tacos, transform this into a salad. Slice the tortillas into strips, spritz them with oil, and air-fry them. Put everything else—the pork, cilantro-onion relish, radishes, and salsa—in a bowl and finish off with the air-fried tortilla strips. Enjoy as is, or add your favorite crunchy lettuces, a handful of herbs, and a few slices of avocado.

STEAMED PORK BELLY

with Butter Kimchi Jam

This dish is a play off of bossam, the Korean pork belly dish. Usually, the pork is boiled or simmered; I take a slightly different approach and cure the belly for a few hours before steaming it. That does mean you have to plan a little ahead for this, but it's a good investment: That little extra time will tenderize the pork while infusing it with some flavor. And even though the pork belly captures the attention, the dish really revolves around all the vegetables and herbs on the platter, which you stack and eat with the pork. On their own and on your own, you'd never eat this quantity of greens, but put a slice of steamed pork belly right on top? Suddenly, you've eaten a big fucking salad. This is great served either hot or cold.

SERVES 6 TO 8

Pork Belly

1 cup Diamond Crystal kosher salt

1 cup sugar

2 pounds pork belly, skin removed

For Serving

Kosher salt

1 head napa cabbage, leaves separated

Butter Kimchi Jam (page 254)

Stack of perilla or shiso leaves

1 bunch scallions, green parts only, cut into 2-inch pieces

Ssamjang dip, homemade (page 59) or store-bought, or any other sauce you'd like (see page 221 for some ideas)

1. *Cure the pork belly:* In a large bowl, combine the salt and sugar. Add the pork belly and rub the salt/sugar mix all over. Cover the bowl, place it in the fridge, and cure it for 2 hours. After 2 hours, remove the pork and rinse it well.

2. Fill a large pot fitted with a steamer basket with water to come up to about 1 inch or so below the basket. Bring to a boil over high heat. Reduce to medium-low and add the pork belly to the basket. Cover and gently steam the pork until it's tender, about 35 minutes.

3. Turn off the heat and let the pork rest in the steamer basket, partially covered with the lid, while you prepare the ingredients for serving.

4. *For serving:* Set up a large bowl of ice and water. Bring a pot of lightly salted water to a boil over high heat. When it hits a boil, drop the napa cabbage leaves into the water and boil for about 30 seconds, then use tongs or a spider to transfer them to the ice bath. Once cooled, remove and dry.

5. If you haven't done so already, make the butter kimchi jam.

6. Remove the pork from the steamer basket. If necessary, cut the pork into strips almost as wide as the cabbage leaves, then cut into ¼-inch-thick slices. Realistically, you and your friends will start eating right then and there, but if you want to plate it nice, place stacks of napa cabbage leaves and perilla or shiso on a platter. Take a handful of scallions and pile it next to the greens, then fan out the slices of pork. Transfer the dipping sauce and kimchi jam to bowls and nestle them in the middle of the platter if you can. Bring everything to the table.

7. For the perfect bite, layer the cabbage and perilla or shiso leaves with a slice of pork belly on top, some kimchi, a scallion or two, and a dollop of sauce and bite.

WRAPPE

A ssam platter is a magic trick. It's a big plate of lots of things going on—vegetables, herbs, some protein, a dip or two—but it's the protein that usually grabs your attention. And as you're looking that way, you miss the real action: all the vegetables and herbs you're using to wrap that little piece of meat into the most perfect bite. By the end of the meal, you've eaten a salad's worth of raw veggies without even thinking about it. I make my ssam platter with pork belly (page 218), but that's just one way to do it. **To build your own:**

Pick a protein

Almost anything will work. For example:

- The roast pork from the Roast Pork Tacos with Salsa Verde (page 216)

- Steak, either from the Kimchi Steak Tacos (page 234) or Steak with Chimichurri (page 230)

- The tofu in the Drunken Kimchi Tofu Sifu (page 116); or lightly sear some firm tofu in a bit of toasted sesame oil

- Crispy.Salmon.Lemon. (page 192)

- Crab Quakes (page 198)

- Shredded roasted chicken; or grab a rotisserie chicken from the market and shred that

- Grilled chicken or pork

Prep some vegetables to wrap up, too, for extra texture and flavor, like say:

- Shredded carrots

- Sliced scallions

- Thinly sliced jalapeños

- Cucumbers, thinly sliced into coins or cut into matchsticks

- Thinly sliced garlic

- Quickles (page 52), cut to fit into a wrap

R'S
ELIGHT

Wrap it up

These all make excellent wrappers. You can get away with having just one type of wrapper on the table, but the more options for stacking, the more options for flavor.

- Napa cabbage leaves
- Perilla or shiso leaves
- Red or green lettuce leaves
- Bibb or butter lettuce
- Iceberg lettuce
- Endive
- Pickled radish wraps, available at Korean markets

Dipping

You gotta have at least one dip to go with this. Any of these will work:

- Korean Ssamjang Dip (page 59); or make a quick version by combining equal parts gochujang and doenjang (soybean paste); or pick up a tub of ssamjang at an Asian market
- Magic Sauce (page 247)
- If you made the Braised Spicy Korean Chicken (page 210) and have any of the braising liquid leftover, that will make for a damn good dip
- Soy-Ginger Sauce (page 244)
- Ginger Ponzu Sauce (page 246)

On the side

Add a few side dishes to round things out:

- Cooked rice
- Butter Kimchi Jam (page 254) or store-bought kimchi
- Quickles (page 52)
- Cold Tofu and Chives with Soy-Ginger Sauce (page 114)
- Korean Steamed Egg Soufflé (page 124)

BRAISED 'N' GLAZED PORK RIBS

These ribs are my version of the sticky BBQ rib appetizer at P.F. Chang's and other Chinese American restaurants. It's also what I would do if I ran a Tony Roma's (a Tony *Roy*ma's, let's say) and didn't have the smoker and the wood and all the rest of the equipment to barbecue baby back ribs. So, to make a nice plate of ribs, I'd do it up with a little bit of technique: first, braising the ribs in a flavorful liquid, then outfitting them in a citrusy, savory, sticky glaze. To save some time, you could make the glaze up to 4 days in advance and store it, covered, in the fridge.

SERVES 4 TO 6 (OR MORE AS PARTY BITES)

Braised Ribs

2 racks baby back ribs

5 ounces fresh ginger, peeled and chopped (an overflowing ½ cup)

1 medium yellow onion, chopped

1 cup whole garlic cloves (30 to 40 cloves), peeled

1 cup cilantro stems

1 cup rice vinegar

2 tablespoons Diamond Crystal kosher salt

2 tablespoons granulated sugar

1 tablespoon black peppercorns

1. *Braise the ribs:* Slice the racks into 5- or 4-rib portions.

2. In a large stockpot, bring 6 quarts water to a boil over high heat. Add the ginger, onion, garlic, cilantro stems, vinegar, salt, granulated sugar, and peppercorns. Cover and return to a boil. Once the water is back at a boil, add the ribs and reduce the heat to medium-low. Cover and simmer for 40 minutes.

3. Uncover the ribs and continue to simmer the ribs until they are cooked through and tender but not yet falling off the bone, 35 to 45 minutes. (A quick word about the braise: You want to let the ribs go long enough that they become tender, but not so long that they fall apart. If they do, they'll overcook when they're glazed and go into the oven.)

4. *Meanwhile, make the glaze:* In a blender, combine 1½ cups water, the orange juice, black bean paste, hoisin, oyster sauce, sambal, lime juice, sriracha, mustard powder, brown sugar, and granulated sugar and puree until smooth.

5. Preheat the oven to 450°F.

6. When the ribs are done braising, set them aside until cool enough to handle, then slice them into individual ribs and place on a wire rack set in a sheet pan.

Glaze

½ cup orange juice

½ cup chunjang (black bean paste; see Note)

½ cup hoisin sauce

¼ cup oyster sauce

¼ cup sambal oelek

2 tablespoons fresh lime juice

2 tablespoons sriracha

1½ tablespoons Chinese mustard powder

1 tablespoon light brown sugar

1½ teaspoons granulated sugar

For Serving

Chopped scallions, for garnish

Toasted sesame seeds, for garnish

7. In a large shallow skillet, bring the glaze to a light boil over medium heat. Working in batches if necessary, add the ribs in a single layer and cook for 2 minutes. Flip and glaze the other side and cook for 4 minutes. Using tongs, pull out the ribs, set them on the rack skin-side up, and repeat with the rest of the ribs.

8. Spoon a little bit more glaze over all the ribs on the rack for good measure, then transfer to the oven and roast for 10 minutes. Don't discard the glaze in the pan—we're not done with it just yet!

9. Baste the ribs with a few more spoonfuls of the glaze and roast until the ribs are so tender that you can nudge the meat away from the bones with a fork or chopstick, about 10 more minutes. Remove from the oven.

10. *To serve:* Pile the ribs high and garnish with scallions and sesame seeds. Put the rest of the glaze in one or more small bowls so anyone can smear some more on their ribs if they want.

NOTE: Chunjang is a smooth paste made from black soybeans that have been fermented in flour and salt, with some caramel added for color and sweetness. You can find tubs and jars of it at any Korean market and many Asian grocers, too.

Power Up

It doesn't take a whole lot of ribs to satisfy, so complete your meal with some flatbread (page 172) and grilled vegetables like Grilled Romaine with Creamy Blue Cheese Dressing (page 94) or Grilled Artichoke and Zucchini (page 70).

Braised 'n' Glazed Pork Ribs 222

Not Shrimp Toast but Think Shrimp Toast, Okay? OK! 226

NOT SHRIMP TOAST BUT THINK SHRIMP TOAST, OKAY? OK!

I've always loved shrimp toast. When I was much younger though, shrimp toast was such a mystery: *How* did that layer of shrimp just appear so suddenly inside a fried sandwich?! Of course, I grew up and realized, hey, it's just pureed shrimp slathered on toast and fried in oil. That's what I do here, too, except instead of shrimp, we're going to use a mix of pork, beef, tofu, and a bunch of green cabbage. It's a bit similar to the filling you'd otherwise use for a dumpling, but I always thought dumpling fillings shouldn't be confined to the dumpling. Let it loose and it could be delicious in other things, too, including, as it turns out, spread on toast, where its loose texture works to our advantage. So, if you've never had shrimp toast, or find it so magical that it's intimidating, this is a great way to demystify it a bit by going through the process of making it yourself and finding yourself open to a whole new world of toasts. With the filling spread on sandwich bread and then quartered to make cute little toasts, this will make plenty and feed a party, a softball team, you get the idea. If you're throwing a small party, I still suggest making the whole batch anyway and freezing the leftover filling. It'll keep for up to 3 months.

MAKES 20 TOASTS (SERVES A PARTY)

4 ounces firm tofu

4 ounces ground pork

4 ounces ground beef

1 cup minced scallions

½ cup finely shredded green cabbage

¼ cup minced fresh ginger

¼ cup minced garlic (12 to 14 cloves)

2 tablespoon toasted sesame seeds

2 tablespoons oyster sauce

1. Place the tofu between a layer or two of paper towels and press down to press out the water (or, if you have a cheesecloth, crumble the tofu, place the crumbles in the cheesecloth, and squeeze the water out). You want to drain as much as water as you can, so repeat with another set of paper towels if you think it's necessary.

2. Crumble the tofu and place it in a large bowl. Add the pork, beef, scallions, cabbage, ginger, garlic, sesame seeds, oyster sauce, sesame oil, soy sauce, vinegar, egg, and pinches of gochugaru and salt and mix to evenly combine.

3. Place a cast-iron skillet or other heavy-bottomed skillet over medium heat. Add a touch of oil. When it begins to shimmer, take a small piece of the filling, flatten it slightly, and add it to the pan. This is your tester; you're going to use this to check the seasoning. Cook until it's no longer pink in the middle, then taste. If needed, reseason the mixture and then make additional tester patties until the seasoning's where you want it to be.

2 tablespoons toasted
    sesame oil

1 tablespoon soy sauce

1 tablespoon rice vinegar

1 large egg

Gochugaru

Salt

Neutral oil, like vegetable or
    corn, for shallow-frying (to
    air-fry, see Power Up)

10 slices white sandwich bread

4. Pour in enough oil to come one-third of the way up the sides of the skillet. After about 2 minutes, pop a bread crumb into the oil. If it starts to sizzle with a bunch of little bubbles, the oil is hot enough; if it doesn't, wait another minute and try again. Fish out the piece of bread and discard.

5. While the oil heats, spread a slice of bread with a thick layer of the filling, about ¾ inch or so. Be sure the filling goes edge to edge, corner to corner. Place a second slice of bread right on top and slice off the crusts. Slice the sandwich into quarters to make 4 squares. Run your knife all around the little sandwich squares to smooth out the filling and seal the edges. Repeat with the remaining mixture and slices of bread.

6. When the oil's hot, add the toasts and shallow-fry until golden brown. Flip over and when that side is golden brown, use your tongs to stand them on their edges and fry. In total, it'll take 7 to 8 minutes to fry the toasts to golden brown and cook the pork.

7. Repeat with the remaining toasts. To serve, pile them all on a platter and pass them around the party.

Power Up

For a better-for-you version of these toasts:

- To air-fry: Preheat an air fryer to 350°F. Spray the toasts with olive or avocado oil and place them in the fryer basket (depending on the size of the basket, you may have to cook the toasts in batches) and air-fry until the pork is cooked through.

- Instead of sandwiching the pork between 2 slices of bread, slather the filling on the side of 1 slice of bread. Add some oil to the skillet and heat over medium. Once the oil begins to shimmer, add the toast, pork-side down. When the pork is cooked through, just a few minutes, flip and toast the bread until golden brown and serve it up.

Kimchi
Philly Cheese-steak

I **really love the** category of sandwiches where it's compact enough that you can take just one bite and get a little bit of everything in that one bite. A Philly cheesesteak is exactly that kind of sandwich. When the craving hits, I like to build my own; I make mine with a blast of acidity from kimchi, and I also use the meat you use for shabu shabu, because it's sliced super, super thin, making it perfect for a cheesesteak. I think it's worth going out of your way to a Korean or Japanese market to pick up a pack, but if you can't get to one, that's fine; use really thinly sliced rib eye instead. Because the beef is so thin, it's pretty delicate, so you want to be gentle with it as you cook it. If you have the time, it helps to freeze the meat briefly (think more along the lines of an Otter Pops level of frozen than an ice cube) so it won't tear so easily. And even though I put the sandwich into an oven to melt the cheese right at the end, you can microwave it for a few seconds instead. And check my Power Up suggestions for a few ideas on how to riff on this recipe to fit you.

MAKES ONE 12-INCH-LONG SANDWICH

1 (12-inch) hoagie roll, preferably Amoroso's brand, split

Unsalted butter, at room temperature

Extra-virgin olive oil

½ pound sliced beef cut for shabu shabu, or very thinly sliced rib-eye steak

Salt and freshly ground black pepper

1 cup thinly sliced yellow onion

⅓ to ½ cup Butter Kimchi Jam (page 254)

1½ teaspoons fresh lemon juice

4 to 6 slices provolone cheese

Cheez Whiz

Minced fresh chives, for garnish

1. Preheat the oven to 500°F.

2. Heat a large skillet over medium-low heat. Slather the inside of the hoagie with butter and add it buttered-side down to the pan to toast.

3. In a medium skillet, heat a drizzle of oil over medium heat. When the oil gets glossy and begins to shimmer, add a single layer of beef to cover the bottom of the pan. Season with salt and pepper. Cook just this one side for 1 minute, undisturbed, then remove the slices to a plate or baking sheet. Repeat with the remaining slices of beef.

4. Add the onions to the pan, season them with a pinch of salt and pepper, and sauté. Once they've soaked up the drippings from the beef, about 1 minute, add the butter kimchi jam and stir for 20 seconds. Return all the beef to the pan. Be gentle—the slices are thin and will tear easily, so take the time to add them one by one to the pan. Cook for about 20 seconds, then carefully flip them to finish cooking. Squeeze in the lemon juice and remove from the heat.

5. Check on the bread. It should be golden brown and toasty by now, or close to it. Place the roll on a baking sheet and layer the beef, onions, and kimchi in the roll. Add the provolone and spread some Cheez Whiz on top. Pop the whole thing into the oven for the cheese to melt, 1 to 2 minutes. The bread should be hot but still soft.

6. Place a large piece of butcher or wax paper on the work surface. Put the cheesesteak right on top, garnish with a handful of chives, and close up the sandwich. Roll it up in the paper, slice it in half, and serve it up.

Power Up

- Make this a meal for two by splitting the sandwich in half and serving it with a salad like Cacio e Pepe Caesar Salad (page 98).

- If you prefer, omit the Cheez Whiz.

- Remove the top bun and serve the cheesesteak open-faced with a salad.

- Remove the bread component altogether and serve the filling over a salad, with grilled vegetables, or stuff it inside a bell pepper or portobello mushroom.

CHIM

One of my favorite ways to use chimichurri is to spoon it over a steak, because it brings so much that you don't need a huge portion of the steak to feel fully satisfied. And that means more room on your plate for other fun things, like Quickles (page 52), Crab Quakes (page 198), Roasted Garlic Carrots (page 74), and a salad like the Cacio e Pepe Caesar Salad (page 98). You also can serve the steak as part of a big ssam platter (see Wrapper's Delight, page 220).

SERVES 4

1 pound rib-eye steak

Salt and freshly ground black pepper

1 cup Chimichurri (page 247)

Extra-virgin olive oil

3 tablespoons unsalted butter

5 garlic cloves, crushed or halved

3 sprigs fresh thyme

1. Season both sides of the steak generously with salt and pepper. Rest the rib eye on the counter for 30 minutes. If you haven't made the chimichurri yet, make it now, because it also should sit for at least 30 minutes to develop flavors.

2. In a large sauté pan or cast-iron skillet, heat 2 tablespoons olive oil over medium-high heat. When it begins to smoke, add the steak. Sear until it forms a nice crust, 3 to 4 minutes. Flip and add the butter, garlic, and thyme sprigs. Carefully tilt the pan and spoon the butter over the steak repeatedly until it's as done as you'd like. I like my steak medium-rare, so that's another 2 to 3 minutes.

3. Place the steak on a cutting board and let rest for 10 to 15 minutes. Slice into thick strips, shingle them on a serving platter, and spoon some of the sauce and garlic from the pan over the slices, then plenty of chimichurri on top (you can discard the thyme sprigs, or use them as garnish). Serve with the rest of the chimichurri in a bowl on the side so everyone can help themselves to more.

STEAK with CHIMICHURRI

SHAKING SALTADO

When I first had shaking beef at a Vietnamese restaurant, years and years ago, I also happened to be eating a lot of lomo saltado, the chifa (Chinese Peruvian) dish. Those two dishes are rooted in two different cultures each with its own unique history, but in my head, I saw a bunch of overlap between them: the beef, the bell peppers, the tomatoes, the greens. Both have a different but similar vinegary sauce. And so, I forever connected the two. This recipe is one that's lived in my head all these years, with flavors from both merged into one (though without the fries you'd usually get with a lomo saltado). Eat this with a bowl of rice or a green salad simply dressed with Dijon Balsamic Vinaigrette (page 102) or tossed with some toasted sesame oil, lemon juice, salt, and pepper.

SERVES 4 TO 6

Sauce
½ cup Chinkiang black vinegar (see Note)

½ cup fish sauce

½ cup sambal oelek

¼ cup fresh lime juice

Beef
Neutral oil, like corn or vegetable oil

16 ounces beef filet or tenderloin, sliced against the grain into ¼-inch-thick strips

Salt and freshly ground black pepper

1 teaspoon toasted sesame oil

2 bunches scallions, cut into 2-inch segments

¼ cup minced fresh ginger

¼ cup minced garlic

1 cup thinly sliced red bell pepper

1 cup thinly sliced yellow onion

Unsalted butter

4 ounces fresh cilantro

4 ounces watercress or arugula

1. *Make the sauce:* In a medium bowl, whisk together the vinegar, fish sauce, sambal, and lime juice. Set aside.

2. *Cook the beef:* In a large skillet, heat 2 to 3 teaspoons oil over high heat. When it begins to shimmer, add the beef, working in batches if necessary to avoid overcrowding the skillet. Season it with salt and pepper and leave it alone for about a minute so they can get a good sear and the beef no longer sticks to the pan. At that point, start moving the beef strips around to get a good sear on all sides, 4 to 5 minutes total. You may start to get a little impatient here, but take the time to sear the beef on all sides; the flavor you get is worth it. Also, you're just looking to sear it here; you don't want to cook it through just yet. Remove the beef to a plate.

3. Add the sesame oil, scallions, ginger, and garlic and toss it all together until fragrant. Add the bell pepper and onion and stir for another 30 seconds. Return the beef to the pan along with the sauce. Toss to coat the beef in the sauce, about 1 minute for medium-rare, or a few minutes longer for medium or well-done. Add a pat of butter.

4. Turn off the heat and transfer everything to a platter or a plate. Add the cilantro and watercress right on top and serve.

NOTE: Chinese black vinegar is an aromatic, malty vinegar made by fermenting rice and grains. Different regions in China produce their own homegrown version; here in the US, the black vinegar from the city of Zhenjiang (or Chinkiang) is the one you'll most often find on the shelves at Asian markets.

Kimchi

STEAK

So, I know I'm the Korean barbecue tacos guy, but these tacos are coming from another part of the Korean constellation of dishes: bibimbap. But rather than topping a bowl of rice with seared beef, kimchi, a bunch of veggies, and a gochujang sauce, we're going to use tortillas as our base instead. Like most street tacos, these are best eaten the second they're made.

MAKES 12 TACOS

2 rib-eye steaks (8 ounces each)

Salt and freshly ground black pepper

Extra-virgin olive oil

2 tablespoons unsalted butter

1½ cups shredded romaine lettuce

1 cup thinly sliced yellow or red onion

1 cup chopped fresh cilantro, leaves and stems

1 cup chopped kimchi

At least 4 limes, halved

24 street taco–sized (4½ inches) corn tortillas

½ to 1 cup Magic Sauce (page 247)

1 bunch scallions, thinly sliced

Salsa Roja (optional; page 251), for serving

1. Place a large skillet, preferably cast-iron, over medium-high heat. While it heats, season both sides of the rib eyes very generously with salt and pepper.

2. Once the skillet is smoking hot, add enough oil to coat the bottom of the pan. Place the rib eyes in the hot pan and sear until a nice crust forms, about 5 minutes. Flip and add the butter. Tilt the pan to collect the butter and spoon it over the steak continuously for 3½ to 4 minutes for medium-rare (you'll know it's medium-rare by pressing the steak with your finger: It should feel the same way it feels as when you press your nose).

3. Remove the rib eyes from the pan and let rest for 5 to 10 minutes.

4. While the rib eyes rest, in a medium bowl, combine the lettuce, onion, cilantro, and kimchi. Season with a pinch of salt and pepper. Squeeze half a lime over the slaw and taste. Squeeze in more lime or add more salt or pepper if you think it needs it. Set aside.

5. Heat a medium or large skillet or griddle over low heat with a kiss of olive oil, or you can grease the skillet with the drippings from the rib eye. Stack 2 tortillas on top of each other and place in the pan. Warm them through and toast them slightly, flipping them a few times so they toast evenly. Place them in a tortilla warmer or on a plate and covered with a clean towel to keep them warm. Repeat with the rest of the tortillas.

RECIPE CONTINUES ON PAGE 236

TACOS

6. Slice off a small piece of a steak and taste to check and adjust the seasoning; if the steak needs more salt or pepper, sprinkle a bit more over the uncut pieces. Slice off the fattier parts of the steak and discard (or save for another use) and cut the rest of the steaks into thin slices.

7. To assemble a taco, place a double stack of tortillas on a cutting board. Add a few pieces of steak, a little bit of the rib eye drippings out of the pan if you want, a spoonful of the Magic Sauce, then the slaw and some scallions. Serve immediately with wedges of lime on the side and bowls of salsa for anyone to add as they wish while you make the rest of the tacos.

CHOICE WORDS: One of the things I wanted to hit on with the short rib taco at our food truck Kogi BBQ was the perfect bite: The one perfect bite that stops you in your tracks, the one perfect bite that gives you a sense of where its flavors traveled to and from to land on that tortilla to make that taco. This book is full of one perfect bites, including this taco, my Kimchi Philly Cheesesteak (page 228), and Shrimp Fried Rice (page 170).

Get In Where You Fit In

If you have any Orange Bang Vinaigrette (page 104) left in the fridge, you can use that instead of the Magic Sauce. Just combine the vinaigrette with the slaw before using it to top the tacos.

Bonus Rounds

If you have any leftover steak slices, throw them in a rice bowl (page 164), tuck them into an onigiri (page 168), or add them to a cold noodle salad (page 152).

Power Up

Omit the tortillas and serve the steak, topped with a bit of Magic Sauce and scallions, over the slaw. Don't forget the salsa if you got it and lime for the table.

SMUSHED BURGERS

As I mentioned in the introduction to this book, nowadays when I'm in the mood for a burger, I'm more likely to make the burger myself, so I can control every part of it, from the quality of the ingredients to how the patties are cooked. This burger is influenced by the simplicity of an In-N-Out or short-order grill burger, the flavors of a New Jersey–style steamed onion burger, and a bit of technique from smashed burgers. And I do mean just a bit of technique: The patty here isn't smashed so thinly that you get super-lacy edges the way they are at some smashed burger joints. Instead, I'm smashing it just enough to gain some good surface area for the patty to caramelize. The real smashing comes after the burger is assembled, so the flavors are mashed together and the burger is easier to eat one-handed. It'll end up crumpled like a dented Corolla, a little broken as it repairs your soul. That's LA for you.

MAKES 4 DOUBLE-PATTY BURGERS

- 2 pounds ground beef (80/20), preferably half chuck and half brisket
- Unsalted butter, at room temperature
- 4 brioche or soft sesame buns, split
- Extra-virgin olive oil or a neutral oil like vegetable or corn
- Salt and freshly ground black pepper
- 2 medium yellow onions, super thinly sliced
- 8 slices cheddar cheese
- Ketchup
- Mustard
- Bread and butter pickles

1. Gently shape the beef into eight 4-ounce patties.

2. Place a heavy skillet, preferably cast-iron, over high heat.

3. As the cast-iron skillet heats, place a medium skillet or sauté pan over medium heat. Spread the butter inside the buns, making sure you butter the entire interior and all around the edges. Place the buns buttered-side down in the pan to toast.

4. Drizzle some oil into the cast-iron skillet. Once it begins to shimmer, generously salt and pepper the top of the patties. Place as many patties as you can in the pan without overcrowding, keeping in mind that you're also going to smash them a bit, so they'll need plenty of space to spread. Using the back of a metal spatula, press down on the patties, moving the spatula so you smash the patty evenly all around—but don't press so hard that you end up smearing the beef. You're looking just to flatten and spread the patties to a size just a little bigger than the size of the buns. Cook for about 2 minutes, then press them again, again going for a little bigger than the size of the buns.

RECIPE CONTINUES ON PAGE 240

5. Cook until the patties have a good crisp around the edges, about 1 more minute. Season the top of the patties generously with salt and pepper and flip. Immediately heap a pile of onions and a slice of cheese on top of each patty, reduce the heat to medium-low, and cover. Cook just until the cheese melts, about 1 minute, then uncover and let the patties finish cooking, uncovered, for 30 more seconds.

6. Remove the buns. They should be toasted and golden all over by now. Stack 2 beef patties on a bottom bun, then swirl a bit of ketchup and mustard right on top. Add a few pickles. Cap it off with the top bun. Then wash your hands and place your fist or the palm of your hand on top of the burger and, with no fear and a lot of confidence, press down to smush the burger.

7. Eat immediately. Get a lot of napkins. Repeat with the remaining patties and assemble the rest of the burgers. Get more napkins.

CHOICE WORDS: One of my dreams is to one day open a burger stand. Just a simple place, with a few stools around a counter, a short menu of really delicious burgers. Part of it is because I grew up in LA, and this is a burger town. That, and burgers are a big part of the Korean American experience here; I grew up eating burgers at spots owned by relatives and family friends. So every burger I make is, in its own way, a little homage to all the Korean and Korean American parents who worked those hard hours to raise their kids on burgers and fries.

Power Up

The great thing about making burgers at home is that you can control everything about it. Some ways you can modify this burger:

- I make these burgers with a double patty, but you can always make yours with just a single patty, or make the patties smaller.

- Turn this into a chicken burger by forming ground chicken into 6-ounce patties. It'll take about 2 minutes per side to cook.

- Replace the brioche buns with crisp leaves of iceberg lettuce.

- Add just 1 slice of cheese instead of 2 for each burger, or no cheese at all.

IT'LL END UP CRUMPLED LIKE A DENTED COROLLA, A LITTLE BROKEN AS IT REPAIRS YOUR SOUL.

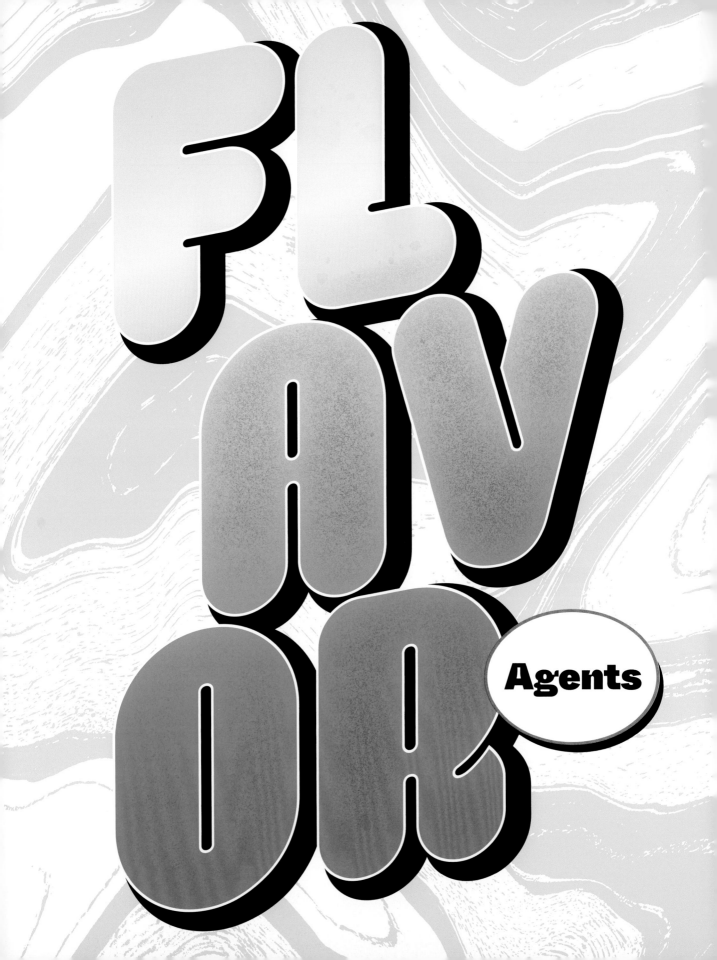

FLAVOR Agents

I know I'm not the only Asian immigrant kid who grew up in a kitchen with a fridge full of trapdoors. Due to frugality and repurposing by Mom Dukes, you just never could trust the labels on the jar or jug. I'd grab a jar of Skippy for my PB&J but find fermented shrimp paste in there instead. Or unscrew the cap of a bottle of yellow Gatorade only to take a huge swig of fish broth. Blahh. And don't get me started on Cool Whip or I Can't Believe It's Not Butter—it definitely wasn't butter, I couldn't believe it—and large tubs of Philly cream cheese. These were her A-list containers.

I was just a kid trying to make a snack, so it took me a while to really understand that what were trapdoors for me were wormholes for my mom. She stocked the fridge full of marinades, kimchis, and dips because she was creating shortcuts for herself. She could come home from a full exhausting day of hustling, pull out those marinades and dips, and go from having nothing on the table to an entire spread in very little time.

And that's what I got for you here: flavor agents, or sauces, marinades, dips, pickles that you can deploy to bring flavor to anything you're eating. These will make it possible for you to quickly round out a meal, make a stir-fry on a Tuesday in less than an hour, have a sauce ready to go with your rice bowl.

Store them in jars and forget to label them. If you do follow my advice, the only wisdom I can share is: Smell before you drink that Gatorade!

GARLIC HERBED BUTTER

This is a compound butter, which sounds fancy, but it just means butter mixed together with one or more ingredients to create a flavored butter. Like here, I'm whisking together butter with garlic and a ton of fresh herbs, and it's going to be so good as a sandwich spread (see The Feel Good Sandwich, page 64) or thrown in with some pasta or rice. Or, if you need to trick yourself and/or your family into eating more whole vegetables, throw a pat of this on some roasted vegetables (like Roasted Cauliflower Steaks, page 78), and I bet they will eat it right up.

MAKES ABOUT 4 OUNCES

8 tablespoons (1 stick) unsalted butter, at room temperature

½ tablespoon minced garlic

¼ cup chopped fresh cilantro

¼ cup chopped fresh basil

¼ cup chopped fresh parsley

¼ cup chopped fresh oregano

Juice of ¼ lemon

Salt and freshly ground black pepper

1 tablespoon extra-virgin olive oil

In a medium bowl, whisk together the butter, garlic, cilantro, basil, parsley, oregano, lemon juice, and a few pinches of salt and pepper. Add the olive oil and whisk again to combine. Serve or refrigerate for up to 1 week, or wrap the butter tightly in plastic wrap and place it in a freezer-safe resealable bag and freeze for up to 6 months.

SOY-GINGER SAUCE

This sauce mimics the ones you get when you order dumplings or boiled beef at a Korean restaurant—but it's not just a dipping sauce. This is also a flavor agent that can be deployed on cold tofu (page 114), added to cooked rice, or spooned into soups. You also can use it as a base to create a multiverse of other sauces by adding chiles and other herbs to it (see Korean Crying Tiger Sauce, page 246). This is something to always have on hand to make snack times and mealtimes that much easier, so make a batch and stash it in the fridge for everyday use.

MAKES 2½ CUPS

1 cup soy sauce

1 cup rice vinegar

2 tablespoons minced fresh ginger

2 tablespoons toasted sesame oil

2 tablespoons toasted sesame seeds

2 tablespoons minced fresh chives

2 tablespoons minced fresh cilantro stems

1 tablespoon chili oil

Juice of ½ lime

Salt and freshly ground black pepper

In a medium pot, combine the soy sauce, vinegar, ginger, sesame oil, sesame seeds, chives, cilantro stems, chili oil, lime juice, 2 tablespoons water, and a pinch of salt and pepper and set over medium-low heat. Increase the heat to high and right when it starts to get goosebumps and bubbles pop all around, 6 to 8 minutes, immediately pull the pot off the heat. Let cool before using. Store in an airtight container in the refrigerator for up to 2 weeks.

Get In Where You Fit In

If you like heat, make a spicy version of this sauce: Take 3 tablespoons of the soy-ginger sauce and mix in 1 tablespoon or more Kimchi Paste (page 255) or sriracha sauce.

FARMERS' MARKET PESTO

One of my earliest claims to fame as a chef was a creamy pesto pasta I made at my first job at a resort in a small California desert town called Borrego Springs. It was one of those times when I felt like I really stuck the landing with every part of the dish, especially the pesto, which I loaded with cheese to up its savoriness and turn it creamy so it could work both as a sauce and a dip. This pesto has stuck with me ever since. There aren't too many ingredients in here, so pick up the best you can get; for me, that means swinging by the farmers' market for the freshest basil and lemons. In fact, if I ever set up shop at the farmers' market, I'd set up with this pesto; you'd walk past the pita and fresh hummus stand called Mom's or Brothers or Sisters and find me right there, free samples for everyone. Now, a "real" pesto is made with a mortar and pestle; mine's made in a blender or food processor, so it's not so much a "real" pesto as it's my un-real pesto.

MAKES ABOUT 2 CUPS

1 cup pine nuts

4 cups fresh basil leaves

1 cup plus 2 tablespoons extra-virgin olive oil

1 cup grated Parmesan cheese

Grated zest and juice of 1 lemon

2 tablespoons minced garlic

Salt and freshly ground black pepper

Pita chips, crostini, bagel chips, or raw veggies, for dipping

1. In a small pan, toast the pine nuts over very low heat until they're fragrant and browned, shaking the pan a few times so they toast evenly. It might feel like it's taking forever to toast, but don't walk away: The nuts go from toasted to burnt real quick. Transfer the toasted nuts to a bowl and cool.

2. In a blender or food processor, combine the cooled nuts, basil, oil, Parmesan, lemon zest, lemon juice, garlic, a fat pinch of salt, and some pepper. Puree until smooth. Stop the blender, taste, adjust the seasoning if necessary.

3. Serve as a dip with pita chips, crostini, bagel chips, or raw veggies. Leftovers can be poured into a jar or airtight container with a thin layer of olive oil on top (to keep the color) and refrigerated for up to 1 week. Or, make a big batch and divide it among all the little cubes in an ice cube tray and freeze. Then pop the cubes out, place them in a resealable bag, and keep 'em in the freezer for up to 6 months.

Bonus Rounds

This pesto makes a great pasta sauce by adding it to a hot pan with just a touch of cream and more shredded Parmesan, but really, it's an everything sauce. Use it to bring some instant flavor to:

- Sandwiches or burgers by adding mayo to the pesto to make a spread

- Salads and greens by combining a dollop of pesto with a few spoonfuls of lemon juice and some olive oil to make a vinaigrette (see page 109 for more on how to make your own vinaigrette)

KOREAN CRYING TIGER SAUCE

This starts with my Soy-Ginger Sauce (page 244) and adds some fish sauce, ginger, lemongrass, Thai bird's eye chiles, and chili garlic sauce. The result is a spicy, savory hybrid of the nước chấm that comes with rice noodles at Vietnamese spots, the ssamjang that you get at Korean BBQ restaurants, and the crying tiger sauce at Thai places.

MAKES ABOUT ½ CUP

¼ cup Soy-Ginger Sauce (page 244)

2 tablespoons fish sauce

2 tablespoons minced lemongrass (see Lemongrass, page 34)

1 tablespoon minced fresh chives

1 tablespoon chopped fresh cilantro

1 tablespoon minced Thai bird's eye chiles

1 teaspoon chili garlic sauce

Juice of ½ lime

Pinch of sugar

In a small pot, combine the soy-ginger sauce, 1 tablespoon water, the fish sauce, lemongrass, chives, cilantro, chiles, chili garlic sauce, lime juice, and sugar and set over medium-low heat. Increase the heat to high and right when you see and hear one thousand tiny bubbles crackle and pop all around the pot, 6 to 8 minutes, remove from the heat. Let cool before using. Store in an airtight container and in the refrigerator for up to 1 week.

GINGER PONZU SAUCE

This ponzu sauce is a super-versatile dip that can keep, refrigerated and covered, for about a week. If you omit the ginger and jalapeño, though, it'll keep even longer, so you can double this up and add those ingredients each time you serve the sauce. The longer the sauce sits, the better it will get.

MAKES 1 CUP

½ cup soy sauce

½ cup rice vinegar

Grated zest and juice of 1 lime

1 tablespoon grated fresh ginger

1 jalapeño, thinly sliced

Salt and freshly ground black pepper

In a bowl, combine ¼ cup water, the soy sauce, vinegar, lime zest, lime juice, ginger, and jalapeño. Stir to combine. Season with salt and pepper to taste. It's ready to go.

CHIMI-CHURRI

Chimichurri is one of the first recipes I explored as a chef, and I really fell in love with how a bunch of chopped fresh vegetables and herbs could be transformed into something so flavorful and punchy. Use it on everything.

MAKES ABOUT 2 CUPS

1 cup extra-virgin olive oil

½ cup red wine vinegar

½ cup chopped fresh parsley

¼ cup minced red onion

¼ cup minced shallots

¼ cup minced garlic (12 to 14 cloves)

¼ cup chopped fresh cilantro

1 tablespoon dried oregano

Crushed red pepper flakes

Salt and freshly ground black pepper

In a large bowl, whisk together the olive oil, vinegar, parsley, onion, shallots, garlic, cilantro, oregano, a pinch of red pepper flakes, and a good pinch of salt and black pepper. Taste and adjust the seasoning if needed. Let it sit at room temperature for 25 to 30 minutes so the flavors can meld. It can be stored, airtight, in your fridge for up to 2 weeks.

MAGIC SAUCE

I grew up with my mom saying this soup or that dish had her magic sauce. But you see, it wasn't ever the same sauce, except it kind of was. That magic sauce changed constantly; it was never the same twice. She was truly concocting magic in her blender. This is my version, and it's my homage to Mom. Like hers, this sauce goes everywhere: It goes with the Cold Bibim Noodle Salad (page 152), but you're going to find it as a dip with steamed pork belly (page 218) and on tacos (Kimchi Steak Tacos, page 234). When you're on your own, spoon it over some roast vegetables or toss it with some rice. Make enough for now and the rest of the week because you're going to use it.

MAKES ABOUT 3 CUPS

1 cup gochugaru

½ cup gochujang

½ cup chopped yellow onion

½ cup beef broth or water

6 tablespoons fish sauce

¼ cup rice vinegar

¼ cup toasted sesame oil

1½ tablespoons chopped garlic

1½ tablespoons soy sauce

In a blender, combine the gochugaru, gochujang, ½ cup water, onion, beef broth, fish sauce, vinegar, sesame oil, garlic, and soy sauce. Puree until smooth, then it's ready to use. Keep it in an airtight jar or container and refrigerate; it'll keep for at least a month. Note that right out of the fridge, it may be a little thick; you can add a splash of water to loosen it up before using.

SWEET GARLIC TERIYAKI SAUCE

If you let it, this sauce can take you many, many places. On one journey, it's a stir-fry sauce (Green Bean and Chicken Stir-Fry, page 202). On another trip, it's a marinade and a glaze for wings (Soy-Garlic BBQ Baked Chicken Wings, page 206). It's best to make it ahead of time, so it's ready to go when you are.

MAKES 3½ CUPS

1¼ cups soy sauce

½ cup rice vinegar

½ cup orange juice

¼ cup pineapple juice

2 serrano peppers, coarsely chopped

½ cup whole garlic (15 to 20 cloves), sliced

½ cup sugar

½ medium yellow onion, sliced

½ cup chopped scallions

1 teaspoon crushed red pepper flakes

1. In a medium pot, combine 1 cup water, the soy sauce, rice vinegar, orange juice, pineapple juice, serranos, garlic, sugar, onion, scallions, and pepper flakes. Bring to a boil over high heat. Reduce to a simmer. Skim the scum from the surface of the liquid with a spoon. Gently simmer until the garlic softens, about 20 minutes. Remove from the heat. It's ready to use.

2. To store it, cool it completely, then pour into an airtight container and refrigerate for up to 1 week. You also can freeze this in clean ice cube trays: Cool the sauce completely, then strain and discard the solids, and pour it into the tray. Frozen, it'll keep for 3 months.

THE TRIO

We have dichotomies in LA. Bloods and Crips. Beach and mountain. Eastside and Westside. And salsa verde and salsa roja. One can't exist without the other. If one is L the other is A.

L.A.

I got both types of salsas for you here, plus a fresh pico de gallo outfitted with some avocado to round things out. Make the trio and you're basically there for a great taco, a great burrito, a great plate of fried eggs, a rice bowl—everything.

Salsa Verde

This is my green machine, a magical intersection where Mexican and Asian flavors meet. It's where you'll find our food truck Kogi BBQ parked every day, all day. It has a very slightly smoky flavor because we char the tomatillos so they blister and relax a bit, but there's tons of brightness, too, from the Thai basil and cilantro and acids like lime juice, mirin, and rice vinegar, plus a nuttiness from sesame seeds. On top of that are more flavors from layering similar but different ingredients like serranos and jalapeños, shallots and onions. You need them all in the same way an orchestra needs the violas and the violins. They bring little levels of echo chambers to create my specific sound and make harmony through what might seem like excess. Serve the whole thing at a party, or use what you need and keep the rest in a covered container in the fridge. Dip into it throughout the week.

MAKES ABOUT 2 CUPS

2 tomatillos, husked and rinsed

2 whole garlic cloves, peeled

1 serrano pepper

½ jalapeño

Grated zest and juice of ½ lime

¼ shallot

1 cup torn fresh cilantro

½ cup fresh Thai basil

½ cup diced yellow onion

¼ cup fresh mint leaves

¼ avocado

¼ cup rice vinegar

¼ cup neutral oil, like corn or vegetable oil

¼ cup extra-virgin olive oil

2 tablespoons mirin

1 tablespoon toasted sesame seeds

Salt and freshly ground black pepper

1. Set a skillet, preferably cast-iron, over medium heat. Add the tomatillos and char them on all sides. This may take a few minutes. By the time you're done, the tomatillos should be charred all over and a little soft. Set them aside to cool.

2. Add the cooled tomatillos to a blender, along with the garlic, serrano, jalapeño, lime zest, lime juice, shallot, cilantro, Thai basil, onion, mint, avocado, vinegar, neutral oil, olive oil, mirin, sesame seeds, and a good pinch of salt and pepper. Puree until smooth. Store in a jar or container in the refrigerator for up to 5 days.

Salsa Roja

This is a smoky, warm salsa that combines my memories of taco stands with the flavors of my childhood, which is why you've got some gochugaru thrown in here along with the California chiles and the chiles de árbol. You can and should pour it over everything: tacos, burritos, eggs, chips. It's ready to go as soon as you blend it silky smooth.

MAKES 3 CUPS

2 California chiles (dried Anaheim chiles; see Get In Where You Fit In)

¼ cup dried chiles de árbol (about ⅓ ounce), stemmed

½ medium yellow onion

¼ cup whole garlic cloves (7 to 10 cloves), peeled

Extra-virgin olive oil

2 tomatoes (any kind as long as they're ripe)

½ bunch cilantro

½ cup fresh lime juice

1 teaspoon crushed red pepper flakes

2 tablespoons Diamond Crystal kosher salt

2 tablespoons freshly ground black pepper

1 tablespoon gochugaru

1 tablespoon ground cumin

1. Preheat the broiler.

2. Spread out the chiles, onion, and garlic on a baking sheet. Drizzle a little bit of olive oil all over, just enough to lightly coat everything, and broil them until pliable and roasty, 2 to 5 minutes. Set aside to cool.

3. Meanwhile, place a large skillet, ideally cast-iron, over medium heat. Add the tomatoes and char them on all sides, 8 to 10 minutes. Transfer the tomatoes to a plate to cool.

4. Place all the cooled chiles, onion, garlic, and tomatoes in a blender and add ½ cup water, the cilantro, lime juice, pepper flakes, salt, black pepper, gochugaru, and cumin. Puree until smooth. Store it in the fridge in an airtight container for up to 10 days. Add tons to everything.

Get In Where You Fit In

If you can't find California chiles, you can use ancho chiles instead.

Pico de Gallo

I generally prefer pureed salsas, but there are times and places when the freshness and crispness of pico de gallo will pull everything on the plate together, like, say, when you have a Bean and Cheese Burrito (page 86) or a fish taco (page 186), or you want a topping for a tray of nachos. For this pico de gallo, I add avocado for a bit of umami and textural contrast, and you can use any tomatoes you have as long as they're ripe. It's best as soon as it's made.

MAKES 2 CUPS

1 cup diced avocado

1 cup diced tomatoes (any kind of tomato as long it's ripe)

1 cup diced yellow onion

½ cup chopped fresh cilantro, stems and leaves

¼ cup fresh lime juice

2 tablespoons minced jalapeño

Salt and freshly ground black pepper

In a medium bowl, mix together the avocado, tomatoes, onion, cilantro, lime juice, jalapeño, and generous pinches of salt and pepper. Serve.

HOW TO KIMCHI ANYTHING

I use *kimchi* as a verb, because that's what it is: It's all action. My Kimchi Paste (page 255) is a magic potion, the ultimate flavor enhancer. Use the paste to kimchi almost anything to eat right away, or add it to a vegetable and let it ferment and develop deep, complex flavors over days or weeks. Kimchi'ing is a great way to use up the fruits and vegetables you haven't gotten to but need to get to.

To kimchi something to eat right now

Take whatever you have, slice it up, and throw it in a bowl. Add a few spoonfuls of the kimchi paste and mix. Taste. Season with salt and pepper if you think it needs it. Eat. That's it. Seriously.

Try kimchi'ing a watermelon (page 54), or apples, Asian pears, melons, cantaloupe, papaya, mango, stone fruit, even oranges. Or kimchi cucumbers or a bunch of scallions or chopped napa cabbage and eat with a bowl of rice or soup.

One more idea: Kimchi thickly sliced ripe tomatoes and plate them with fresh basil and mozzarella for a new-school caprese salad.

To kimchi something to eat later

Some vegetables, like napa cabbage and daikon radishes, connect with something deep in your soul when you add the paste and let them ferment for a few days or even weeks. Depending on the vegetable, you'll need to salt or brine it in a saltwater solution before applying the paste. There are a ton of guides out there that can walk you through that exact process. After setting it aside to ferment, remember to taste it every day until you feel that soul connection. Then, fridge it and dip into it for every meal. Kimchi goes with everything.

Fruit kimchis are best eaten right away because the longer the fruit sits in the paste, the more they'll soften, break down, and lose their texture and crunch. But if life happens and you kimchi a fruit that you can't eat right away, I'd put it in an airtight container and set it aside on the counter to ferment. Taste it every few hours, and when it tastes good to you, puree the whole thing in a blender and use it as a condiment. Or, blend in some chiles and turn it into a hot sauce.

Butter Kimchi Jam

MAKES ABOUT 1½ CUPS

Kimchi is always great on its own, but warm it up with a little bit of butter and sesame oil and it becomes a brand-new side dish. It's great with everything from tofu to pork, and it can be served at room temperature or even cold right out of the fridge.

Toasted sesame oil

Generous 1 tablespoon unsalted butter

2 cups chopped kimchi, plus ¼ cup kimchi juice

Salt and freshly ground black pepper

½ cup minced scallions

1 tablespoon toasted sesame seeds

In a small pan, pour in enough sesame oil to coat the bottom of the pan and set over medium-low heat. Add the butter and when it starts to foam, brown, and smell a little nutty, add the chopped kimchi. Season with salt and pepper. Stir until the kimchi softens and lightly caramelizes, 5 to 10 minutes. Add the kimchi juice, scallions, and sesame seeds and remove from the heat. Taste, adjust the seasoning, and it's ready to go. To store, cool it completely, then transfer to an airtight container and refrigerate for up to 1 month.

Kimchi Paste

MAKES 3½ TO 4 CUPS

This is an all-purpose paste that deserves a permanent spot in your fridge next to the salsas, sriracha, and pestos. You can use it, of course, to kimchi anything, but it's also a bridge between recipes. Add it to any fried rice to transform your bowl. Spoon a bit into a dip like the Soy-Ginger Sauce (page 244) to make an entirely new spicy sauce. Or stir some into a soup like Oxtail Brisket Soup (page 146) and it will turn one recipe into two.

1 cup gochugaru

1 cup chopped yellow onion

1 cup chopped scallions

½ cup whole garlic cloves
   (15 to 20 cloves), peeled

¼ cup chopped peeled fresh ginger

¼ cup rice vinegar

¼ cup soy sauce

2 tablespoons Diamond Crystal
   kosher salt

2 tablespoons sugar

1. In a blender, combine the gochugaru, onion, scallions, garlic, ginger, vinegar, soy sauce, ¼ cup water, the salt, and sugar and blend until smooth. It'll be a thick puree, so stop the blender every once in a while to stir the mixture and scrape down the sides of the container. If the mixture is *too* thick, add a splash of water here and there as necessary. When blended, the paste should be about as thick as a hummus or harissa.

2. Transfer the paste to an airtight container and refrigerate for up to 1 month.

To YOUNG ROY

It took me a life's journey to get to a point where I felt like I could share this with you. And by "you" I mean me, too—this book is a book I wish I could have given a younger version of myself, when I was lost and confused and didn't know where I fit in or how to fit in. I wanted to leave you with a few thoughts to take with you on your cooking and life journey:

1

The more you cook from the heart and tell the smaller, more singular story, the more it will connect with others.

2

Use your anger to bring peace to this world.

3

Share and feed others with love.

4

Don't change but evolve.

5

The flavors you love will be the flavors that others will love, too.

6

Being yourself and making food that looks and tastes like nothing else out there is not a crime. It's invention!

7

Being yourself and not conforming doesn't mean being disrespectful, as others may lead you to believe.

8

The moment you try to be everything to everybody is when you are at your weakest.

9

There is no middle America, we are all spilling over the edges. Don't be brainwashed by the cacophony of dumbshit media.

10

Skateboarding is not a crime.

11

You're not in trouble.

12

Be honest, don't cut corners. You can taste fraud.

13

Bring light, but dwell in the darkness to strengthen that light.

14

Food connects us all but it can be used to separate us and label us. Fight through that shit and know what you're about.

15

Listen when people criticize, but stay true. Let it settle within you, then apply and adapt.

16

Popular belief doesn't mean all truths. There are truths around food, access, health that only you can interpret because you lived it and are sensitive to the disparity. Don't let people ever try to convince you otherwise.

17

The world is unfair and you know there are rungs on the ladder of struggle. Honor that no matter what the intellectual world tells you.

18

Double down on love and positivity.

19

Be on time and always give it your all.

20

Take it all with a grain of salt.

START HERE . . .

if you don't know where to start

The recipes in this book are designed for you to just start cooking: Find whatever looks good to you and go. But, if you need a little direction or some ideas for a themed dinner party, I got you.

Tuesday Night Dishes for the Family

If you're looking to pull together something quick for the family, these are sides and mains that don't require too much prep or can be made pretty quickly, or both! And if you have time to make more than one dish, play mix and match. You can't lose.

Vegetables

- Roasted Garlic Carrots with Broken Orange Vinaigrette (page 74)
- Roasted Beets with Chili Crisp, Cilantro, and Lime (page 76)
- Stir-Fried Pea Shoots with Garlic and Chiles (page 68)
- Calabrian Chile Broccoli Rabe (page 66)

Soups

- Bomb Kha Chowder (page 138)
- Creamy Orzo Chicken Soup (page 136)
- Egg Drop Top Soup (page 130)

Rice and pasta

- Clam I Am Pasta (page 154)
- Shakshuka Baked Ziti (page 160)

Seafood and meats

- Roast Pork Tacos with Salsa Verde (page 216)
- Pssstcado the Unfried Fish Taco (page 186)
- Hawaiian-Style Garlic Shrimp (page 194)
- Turmeric-Steamed Mussels (page 191)
- Green Bean and Chicken Stir-Fry (page 202)

. . . and a few easy side dishes to round out your meal

- Quickles (page 52)
- Butter Kimchi Jam (page 254)
- Cold Tofu and Chives with Soy-Ginger Sauce (page 114)
- Drunken Kimchi Tofu Sifu (page 116)

THE CHOI OF COOKING

Snacks

If you want to just satisfy your munchies, any of these will do the trick.

For a sweet snack

- Smooth Operator (page 49)
- Watermelon Kimchi (page 54)

For a savory snack

- Cold Tofu and Chives with Soy-Ginger Sauce (page 114)
- Egg Drop Top Soup (page 130)
- Deviled Egg Sandos (page 128)

For a crunchy snack

- Watermelon Kimchi (page 54)
- Farmers' Market Pesto (page 245) with pita chips or rice crackers for dipping
- Crudités with your choice of dip (page 56)
- Chicken Nuggs (page 208)

For a study-time snack

- Crispy Mashed Potatoes (page 82)
- Ohh-nigiri (page 168)
- Cold Bibim Noodle Salad (page 152)

Tailgate Party

These are small bites talking big game: They can be easily scaled up for a tailgate or picnic, and you can eat them with one hand and a foam finger on the other.

- Watermelon Kimchi (page 54)
- Crudités with Roasted Eggplant and Tomato Dip (page 58) or Korean Ssamjang Dip (page 59)
- Big Fucking Salad with Dijon Balsamic Vinaigrette (page 90)
- Pico de Gallo (page 251)
- Salsa Verde (page 250)
- Salsa Roja (page 251)
- Not Shrimp Toast but Think Shrimp Toast, Okay? OK! (page 226)
- Chicken Nuggs (page 208)
- Soy-Garlic BBQ Baked Chicken Wings (page 206)
- Steamed Pork Belly with Butter Kimchi Jam (page 218)

Asian Takeout Night

Choose one or two or three of these to make a spread of dishes you might otherwise order for takeout. Whatever you choose, serve it up with some steamed rice.

- Quickles (page 52)
- Crudités with Roasted Eggplant and Tomato Dip (page 58)
- Calabrian Chile Broccoli Rabe (page 66)
- Stir-Fried Pea Shoots with Garlic and Chiles (page 68)
- Cold Tofu and Chives with Soy-Ginger Sauce (page 114)
- Egg Drop Top Soup (page 130)
- Veggie on the Lo Mein Spaghetti (page 158)
- Shrimp Fried Rice (page 170)
- Green Bean and Chicken Stir-Fry (page 202)
- Black Pepper Taiwanese-Style Pork Chops (page 214)
- Shaking Saltado (page 232)

Couch Potato

These are easy, low-effort things to make when it's just you and a good low-stakes, high-drama drama to binge, or when it's just one of those days you find it hard to get off the couch.

- Smooth Operator (page 49)
- Tuna Salad Niçoise Bibimbap (page 92)
- Korean Steamed Egg Soufflé (page 124)
- Underwear Rice Bowl (page 164)
- Ohh-nigiri (page 168)
- Cold Bibim Noodle Salad (page 152)
- Hawaiian-Style Garlic Shrimp (page 194)
- Green Bean and Chicken Stir-Fry (page 202)
- Black Pepper Taiwanese-Style Pork Chops (page 214)
- Soy-Ginger BBQ Baked Chicken Wings (page 206)
- Smushed Burgers (page 239)

ACKNOWLEDGMENTS

This book was a lifetime in the making, and there's no way we could have done it by ourselves.

All three of us—Roy, Natasha, and Tien—would like to extend a deep, heartfelt thanks and love to anyone and everyone who went out of their way to lend us a hand, give invaluable feedback, offer moral support, or otherwise contributed to these pages. This book is yours, too.

A FEW PEOPLE WE'D LIKE TO SPECIFICALLY THANK:
Bobby Fisher, for joining us again on this ride, and John Cogan, for your continued support.

Everyone on the photography production: Caroline Hwang and Nidia Cueva, thank you for your creative and artistic vision and guidance. And our wonderful crew, thanks for your positive energy and tireless efforts: Dennis Lin, Alex Woods, Sunny Cho, Jesse Ramirez, and Eddie Barrera. Special shout-out to Renée Anjanette, Noah Naylor, and Joshua Kalmar at the Historic Hudson Studios, Alicia Buszczak at The Surface Library, the Hollywood Farmers' Market, K&K Ranch, and all the other farmers' market vendors.

Our OG culinary team who were with us from the very beginning: Sunny Cho, Kumi Megumi, and Todd Chang. We so appreciate your attention to detail and helping us bring these recipes to life.

Our team at Clarkson Potter, including our editor, Jennifer Sit: Thanks for being with us side by side, line by line, to help us shape the book. And thanks, too, to Elaine Hennig, Kate Slate, Rita Madrigal, Lisa Brousseau, Jay Kreider, and everyone else on editorial.

The book production, design, and art are all thanks to a great team, including Serena Wang, Phil Leung, Ian Dingman, Stephanie Huntwork, Laura Palese, and Adela Qersaqi. And thank you to the marketing and publicity team, including Chloe Aryeh, Jina Stanfill, and Kristin Casemore.

Our agents Anthony Mattero and Cindy Uh at Creative Artists Agency, who were more than just agents: Thanks for always being there for us and having our backs from day 1. We're grateful for your loyalty and overall badassery. Thanks, too, to Jamie Stockton and assistants Sydney Shiffman and Naira Mirza.

Clara Bottoms. There aren't enough words. Thank you for everything.

Our families and friends, for being with us every step of the way. Everything you've contributed and everything we've done together lives within this book as well.

Kogi BBQ, for changing our lives, especially Roy's.

Finery LA, for their beautiful aprons.

Our constellation of inspirations, including Los Angeles, Orange County, immigrant restaurants, libraries, independent bookstores and organizations, our earth, the plants and animals we eat, *The Joy of Cooking*, Bruce Lee, and that evil voice in our heads.

Finally, all of YOU: the community who have eaten our food at Kogi BBQ, Best Friend, and beyond; stood in lines; stayed loyal; read our first book; watched our shows; written about, vlogged, and reviewed our places and spaces. THANK YOU!

INDEX

NOTE: Page references in *italics* indicate photographs.

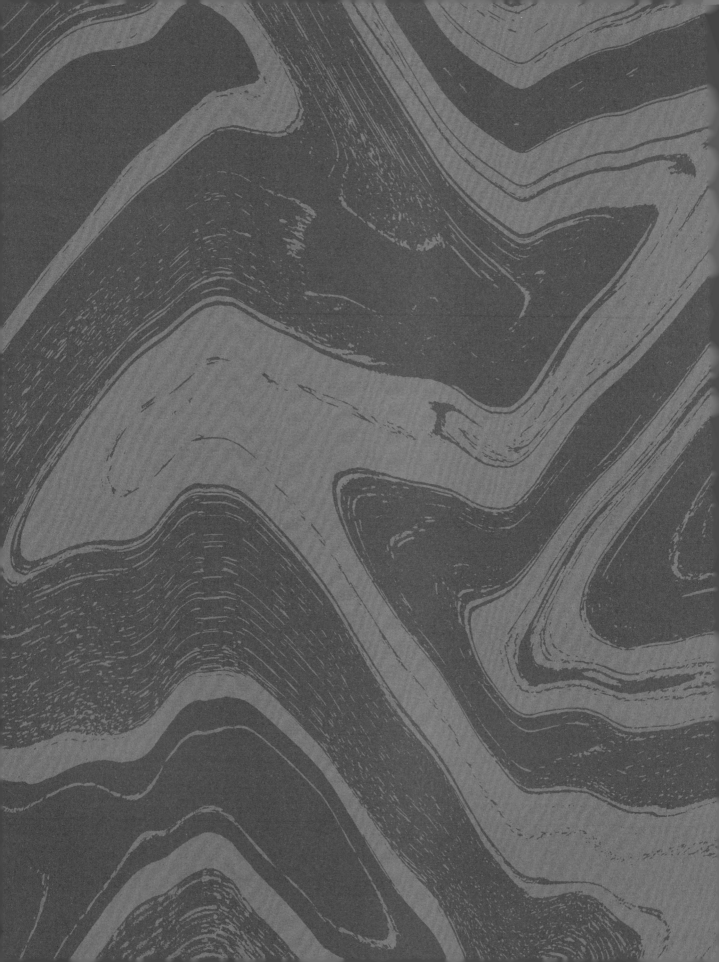